AA

50 Walks in

SCOTTISH HIGHLANDS & ISLANDS

First published 2003
Researched and written by Ronald Turnbull

Produced by AA Publishing
© Automobile Association Developments Limited 2003
Illustrations © Automobile Association Developments Limited 2003
Reprinted 2005

Published by AA Publishing (a trading name of Automobile Association Developments
Limited, whose registered office from 1 October 2005 is Fanum House, Basing View,
Basingstoke, Hampshire, RG21 4EA; registered number 1878835)

OS Ordnance Survey This product includes mapping data licensed from Ordnance Survey®
with the permission of the Controller of Her Majesty's Stationery Office.
© Crown copyright 2005. All rights reserved. Licence number 399221

ISBN-10: 0-7495-3628-4
ISBN-13: 978-0-7495-3628-2

A02701

A CIP catalogue record for this book is available from the British Library. The contents of
this book are believed correct at the time of printing. Nevertheless, the publishers cannot be
held responsible for any errors or omissions or for changes in the details given in this book
or for the consequences of any reliance on the information it contains. This does not affect
your statutory rights. We have tried to ensure accuracy in this book, but things do change
and we would be grateful if readers would advise us of any inaccuracies they may
encounter.

We have taken all reasonable steps to ensure that these walks are safe and achievable by
walkers with a realistic level of fitness. However, all outdoor activities involve a degree of
risk and the publishers accept no responsibility for any injuries caused to readers whilst
following these walks. For more advice on walking safely see page 128. The mileage range
shown on the front cover is for guidance only – some walks may exceed or be less than these
distances.

Visit the AA Publishing website at www.theAA.com/bookshop
Paste-up and editorial by Outcrop Publishing Services Ltd, Cumbria for AA Publishing
Colour reproduction by LC Repro
Printed in Italy by G Canale & C SPA, Torino, Italy

Legend

←-------	Walk route	🅿	Car park
••••••	Optional walk route	〰〰	Cliff
-------	Adjoining footpath	🪨	Rock outcrop
—·—·—	County boundary	〰	Beach
᠕᠅	Viewpoint	🌲🌸	Woodland
▲ 392	Spot height		Parkland
🗺	Built-up area	†	Church, cathedral, chapel
●	Place of interest	WC	Toilet
△	Steep section	🎋	Picnic area

Scottish Highlands & Islands locator map

Contents

Contents

Rating: Each walk is rated for its relative difficulty compared to the other walks in this book. Walks marked 𝝐𝝐 𝝐𝝐 𝝐𝝐 are likely to be shorter and easier with little total ascent. The hardest walks are marked 𝝐𝝐 𝝐𝝐 𝝐𝝐 .

Walking in Safety: For advice and safety tips ➤ 128.

Introducing Scottish Highlands & Islands

The mountains of Scotland come in various shapes. There are the green friendly fells of Perthshire, where the great River Tummel winds idly in its oak-tree gorge and salmon flash in the pools of Killiecrankie. There are the grim crags of Glen Coe – oppressive and even scary on days of low cloud, wind and beating rain. When the clouds do lift and the sun comes out, it's still oppressive and scary because you can see just how high it all goes – back between the crags and above the waterfalls, far back, are icy gullies and a patch of summer snow.

Northwards we come into the Cairngorm massif. These hills are huge but rounded, where the plover cries like a bewildered soul above the fields of boulders. Down around the feet of the Cairngorms the great forest grows, once haunted by bears and wolves, brigands and fairies and broken men. It's tamer today, with the red squirrels and the tourists with

their flasks and sandwiches. Again a great river flows through it, on a bed of golden shingle.

And so we reach the wilds of Wester Ross, where the sea runs in among the mountains. A wide, golden beach, a cragged headland, an ancient dun, and out in the bay, the swift gleam of a porpoise – or was it a whale? After 18 hours of daylight the sun goes down behind a jaggy horizon that has to be the Isle of Skye. Skye, where the bog is boggiest, the midges are mightiest and the pointy purple mountains rise into a blue sky. (Or don't, because the cloud's down – so simply hop across to gentle Raasay.)

In those heather glens of the Grampians, and the green glens of the west, lived a people whose tribal lifestyle was basically Iron Age right up to 1746. The clansmen have left behind their castles in the lochs and their summer huts high on the flanks of the hills. Above all, they've left their stories. Those stories are mostly sad ones: Glen Coe and Culloden, Rob Roy and Bonnie Prince Charlie, and Fingal who roamed the mountain tops before the start of history and played leapfrog across the Glenelg narrows.

Today we have it easy. When it rains, we put on our waterproof jackets and when it snows we go home. Nobody's going to descend out of Rannoch with a broadsword to murder us and steal our cows. But in a way it's the same old story – of pride and poverty, of the fierce love of the home hills. Instead of claymore and fire, the

---

PUBLIC TRANSPORT ⓘ

The Highland railway lines are among the most beautiful in the world – but, apart from the main line north to Inverness, the service is slow and infrequent (Scotrail – national rail enquiries 08457 48 49 50; www.scotrail.co.uk). There is, however, a very useful coach service (Scottish Citylink 08705 50 50 50; www.citylink.co.uk) from Edinburgh and Glasgow to Glencoe, Fort William and Skye. Local buses and postbuses run once a day up many of the glens, while frequent CalMac ferries run to Mull, Iona and Raasay (www.calmac.co.uk).

instruments of plunder are the bulldozer and the planning application. Hordes of humans versus the natural world – it's as fundamental as Highlander versus the King in Edinburgh or London. Let's hope we can solve it without Glen Coe or Culloden this time around.

In this book you'll find a couple of summits – but mostly these are the coastal walks, the forest walks, the walks that go around instead of up the hills, or through the passes, or along the great rivers. Even so, the paths here are harder than in the rest of Britain. Some are peaty trods, unchanged since the days of the cattle drovers. The way will be more tiring than you think, and the higher and longer ones need to be treated with respect (➤ Safety Notes on page 128).

And if your feet are in a bog – though mostly these walks are chosen so they won't be, but if they are – who cares? The rest of you is in the bleak or leafy, the sea-beaten, crag-hanging, faery-haunted Highlands of Scotland.

Using this Book

Information panels

An information panel for each walk shows its relative difficulty (➤ 5), the distance and total amount of ascent. An indication of the gradients you will encounter is shown by the rating ▲▲ ▲▲ ▲▲ (no steep slopes) to ▲▲ ▲▲ ▲▲ (several very steep slopes).

Maps

There are 30 maps, covering 40 of the walks. Some walks have a suggested option in the same area. The information panel for these walks will tell you how much extra walking is involved. On short-cut suggestions the panel will tell you the total distance if you set out from the start of the main walk. Where an option returns to the same point on the main walk, just the distance of the loop is given. Where an option leaves the main walk at one point and returns to it at another, then the distance shown is for the whole walk. The minimum time suggested is for reasonably fit walkers and doesn't allow for stops. Each walk has a suggested map. Laminated aqua3 maps are longer lasting and water resistant.

Start Points

The start of each walk is given as a six-figure grid reference prefixed by two letters indicating which 100km square of the National Grid it refers to. You'll find more information on grid references on most Ordnance Survey maps.

Dogs

We have tried to give dog owners useful advice about how dog friendly each walk is. Please respect other countryside users. Keep your dog under control, especially around livestock, and obey local bylaws and other dog control notices.

Car Parking

Many of the car parks suggested are public, but occasionally you may find you have to park on the roadside or in a lay-by. Please be considerate when you leave your car, ensuring that access roads or gates are not blocked and that other vehicles can pass safely. Remember that pub car parks are private and should not be used unless you have the owner's permission.

The Hill with the Hole

Looking along Loch Awe from Cruachan Reservoir, Britain's biggest energy storage system.

•DISTANCE•	2 miles (3.2km)
•MINIMUM TIME•	1hr 45min
•ASCENT / GRADIENT•	1,200ft (365m) ▲▲▲
•LEVEL OF DIFFICULTY•	🥾🥾 🥾🥾 🥾🥾
•PATHS•	Steep rugged paths, 2 ladder stiles
•LANDSCAPE•	Wooded slopes and high corrie
•SUGGESTED MAP•	aqua3 OS Explorer 377 Loch Etive & Glen Orchy
•START / FINISH•	Grid reference: NN 078268
•DOG FRIENDLINESS•	Good, but high and steep ladder stiles to negotiate
•PARKING•	Two pull-ins on north side of A85, opposite visitor centre. Also lay-by ½ mile (800m) west. Not visitor centre car park
•PUBLIC TOILETS•	Cruachan Visitor Centre

BACKGROUND TO THE WALK

The Cruachan Reservoir collects rainfall from a fairly small catchment, just 9 square miles (23sq km) bounded by the rocky ridge of Ben Cruachan. Even with Cruachan's 116in (2,945mm) of rain a year, the power it produces still only generates about 4 megawatts of power, not quite enough to supply Oban, to the west.

The Big Battery

But Cruachan is more than just a rather small power station. It's a rechargeable storage system for electrical energy, a very big electric battery. The demand for electric power varies from day to day, and even from minute to minute. There's the surge at the advertising break during your favourite soap, as a million kettles get switched on at once. Coal and oil power stations can be stoked up or cooled off, but only quite gradually. Nuclear stations run at the same rate day and night. And the greenest energy sources, wind and wave generators, give power according to the weather. So there has to be a way of taking electricity out of the National Grid when there's too much, and putting it back when it's most needed.

Cruachan Power

Fortunately, an electric generator running backwards becomes a motor, and a turbine turns into a pump. At 'white-meter' (off-peak) times of day, water is pumped from Loch Awe up to Cruachan Reservoir, 1,000ft (305m) above. And at 7:15 on a weekday evening, it flows back down again.

The stored energy in the battery of your car is sufficient to keep it running for about half a minute, but that's enough to start it in the morning and run the tape deck when the engine's off. Full to the brim, Cruachan Reservoir, with the capacity of about half a billion car batteries, in theory holds enough potential energy to supply the UK's peak demand for 10 minutes. In fact the water can't be drawn down that fast, but at full flow Cruachan can supply 400 megawatts, enough for most of Glasgow. Time your arrival for 7:15PM, and you could see the reservoir sinking at an inch (2.5cm) per minute. The same amount of water will be flowing out into Loch Awe, just beside the visitor centre. The whole process – pumping up and then retrieving the potential energy – is not much more than 50 per cent efficient. The waste heat ends up in Loch Awe, where it benefits the fish farm opposite the visitor centre.

The Secret Source

The Cruachan powerhouse makes a fairly small impact on the outer world. Around 12 miles (19km) of pipes bring water into the reservoir, and the outgoing or incoming electricity loops across the hill on high pylons. The 1,030ft (315m) dam is only visible once you reach the corrie; the power station itself is actually buried deep in the heart of the mountain.

Walk 1 Directions

① Two paths run up on either side of the **Falls of Cruachan**. Both are initially rough and steep through woodland. The western one starts at a tarred lane opposite the entrance to the power station proper (not the visitor centre, slightly further to the west). This diminishes to a track, which becomes rough and crosses the railway as a level crossing. A path continues uphill in steep zig-zags through birch, rowan and oak. There are various points to stop and take a look along **Loch Awe**, which disappears glittering into the distance. White speckled stones in the path bed are Cruachan granite. The path continues steeply to the top of the wood.

WHERE TO EAT AND DRINK ℹ

There's a **café** at the Cruachan visitor centre serving refreshments during its opening hours. Oban has a wide selection of cafés, restaurants and pubs looking out over the harbour. The **Falls of Lora Hotel**, at Connel Bridge, has a bistro offering everything from fish and chips to venison and oysters (no dogs allowed). Watch out for Loch Etive's seals and otters as you eat.

---

② Here a high ladder stile crosses a deer fence. With the stream on your right, continue uphill on the small path to a track below the **Cruachan dam**. Turn left, up to the base of the dam, which measures 1,030ft (315m) wide and 150ft (46m) high. Because it's tucked back into the corrie, it can't be seen from below, but it is clearly visible from the top of Dun na Cuaiche (▶ Walk 3), 12 miles (19.3km) away. The hollows between the 13 huge buttresses send back a fine echo. Steps on the left lead up below the base of the dam, then iron steps take you on to the dam's top.

③ From here you look across the reservoir and up to a skyline that's slightly jagged at the back left

corner, where Ben Cruachan's ridge sharpens to a rocky edge. In the other direction, your tough ascent is rewarded by a long view across the low country of Lorn. Turn right to the dam end, where a track leads down right to a junction, then right for 50yds (46m).

④ At this point you could stay on the track to cross the stream just ahead, leading to the top of the path used for coming up. You might wish to do this if you are concerned about the ladder stile on the main route. There is no clear path as you go down to the left of the stream, to reach this high, steep and slightly wobbly ladder stile. Below this there is a clear path that descends grassy slopes and gives a good view of some of the **Falls of Cruachan**. Inside the wood, the path becomes steep and rough for the rest of the way down. Just above the railway, it turns to the left, then passes under the line by a low tunnel beside **Falls of Cruachan Station**, to reach the **A85** below.

WHILE YOU'RE THERE ℹ

From the visitor centre, you can pass by underground tunnels to the vast chamber of the **Machine Hall**, which houses the power station's four turbines. At this point you're about ¾ mile (1.2km) into the mountain, and 1,000ft (305m) below the reservoir. Waste heat from the turbines, as well as plenty of electricity for lighting, means that subtropical plants are able to thrive in this technological underworld.

WHAT TO LOOK FOR ℹ

From the mountain slope you look down the length of **Loch Awe** to its distant outflow – except that you don't. Loch Awe is a reversed lake. Since the ice age, the original outflow at the southern end has silted up and raised the water level to the point where a new outlet formed at the north western corner. As the descent from here to the sea is fairly steep, a small gorge has formed. This has lowered the lake level and eliminated the original outflow altogether.

The Holy Island of St Columba

A circuit of Iona to the marble quarry and the saint's landing place in Coracle Bay.

·DISTANCE·	5¼ miles (8.4km)
·MINIMUM TIME·	3hrs 30min
·ASCENT / GRADIENT·	650ft (198m)
·LEVEL OF DIFFICULTY·	
·PATHS·	Tracks, sandy paths, some rugged rock and heather
·LANDSCAPE·	Bare gneiss rock and Atlantic Ocean
·SUGGESTED MAP·	aqua3 OS Explorer 373 Iona, Staffa & Ross of Mull
·START / FINISH·	Grid reference: NM 286240
·DOG FRIENDLINESS·	On leads near sheep
·PARKING·	Ferry terminal at Fionnphort on Mull
·PUBLIC TOILETS·	Beside Martyr's Bay Bar

BACKGROUND TO THE WALK

In the early summer of AD 563, a middle-aged cleric crossed over from Ireland with 12 companions and the intention of setting up a monastic community on the remote and windswept island of Iona.

Flight of the Dove
Columba (in Gaelic, Colum Cille, the Dove of the Church) did not intend to bring Christianity to a new country, indeed he had left his native Ireland under a cloud. It had started with a dispute over copyright: Columba had secretly copied a psalter owned by St Finnian of Clonard, and Finnian had claimed ownership of the copy. The dispute became more complicated when a young prince accidentally killed an opponent during a game of Irish hockey and claimed sanctuary with Columba. A battle followed, for which Columba felt responsible. It was in penance for these events that he accepted 'white martyrdom', or perpetual exile.

Irish Poetry
At the centre of Columba's settlement on Iona was a church of oak logs and thatch and, around it, huts for the individual monks. Columba himself slept on the bedrock with a stone for a pillow. Larger huts of wattle were used as the dining hall, guest house, library and writing room. The monks' lives consisted of prayer, simple farming and study, and here Columba composed poetry in Latin and Irish.

Celtic Calendar Calculations
Columba's Celtic Christianity spread from Iona across Scotland, and led to the Northumbrian foundation of Lindisfarne, with its rich tradition of illustrated documents such as the *Lindisfarne Gospel*. Here it came into contact with the Roman-style Christianity of continental Europe, brought to England by Augustine in AD 597. While the outward

dispute was on the correct hairstyle for monks and the way to calculate the date of Easter, it seems that the Celtic Christianity was more personal and mystical, the Roman more authoritarian. The Roman version eventually dominated, but the Celtic was never suppressed. Columba, never officially canonised as a saint, is venerated in Scotland and Ireland to this day.

Iona Today

Columba's church vanished beneath a later Benedictine abbey, itself heavily restored in the 19th century. But the spirit of Columba still dominates the island. From the low hill called Dun I, on the day of his death, he blessed the island and community. The monks grew kale and oats at the machars (coastal lowlands) of Bay at the Back of the Ocean (Camus Cuil an t-Saimh), over what is today the golf course. At the southern tip of the island is Coracle Bay, traditionally named as the saint's landing place.

'That man is little to be envied, whose patriotism would not gain force upon the plain of Marathon, or whose piety would not grow warmer among the ruins of Iona,' said the renowned English writer and critic Samuel Johnson, who visited the island in 1773. Today's Iona Foundation is ecumenical – tied to no single denomination of Christianity – and has restored the buildings within a tradition of simple craftsmanship and prayer. The grave of John Smith, Labour leader in the 1990s, lies in the north east extension of the burial ground.

Walk 2 Directions

① Ferries cross to Iona about every hour. Once on the island, take the tarred road on the left, passing **Martyr's Bay**. After a second larger bay, rejoin the road as it bends right. Follow the road across the island to a gate on to the Iona golf course (dogs on leads).

② Take the sandy track ahead, then bear left past a small cairn to the shore. Turn left along the shore to a large beach. At its end, bear left up a narrow valley. After 100yds (91m) you pass a small concrete hut to join a stony track. It passes a fenced reservoir and drops to the corner of **Loch Staoineig**. Walk along to the left of the lochan on a path, improved in places, that runs gently down to **Coracle Bay**. You cross to the left of an area that shows the furrows of lazybed cultivation – fields drained to improve crop yields – and reach the shore just to the left of a rocky knoll.

③ The route ahead is pathless and hard. If your ferry leaves in two hours time or earlier, return by the outward route and leave the marble quarries for another visit. Otherwise, return inland for 200yds (183m) and bear right into a little grassy valley. After 100yds (91m), go through a broken wall and bear slightly left, past another inlet on the right. Cross heather to the eastern shoreline of the island. Bear

left, above the small sea cliff, for ¼ mile (400m). Turn sharp right into a little valley descending to the remnants of the **marble quarry**.

> **WHILE YOU'RE THERE** ℹ
> From Iona, or Fionnphort at the Mull end of the ferry, you can take an open boat trip to the island of Staffa to visit **Fingal's Cave** and its weird basalt formations. The crossing inspired an overture by Mendelssohn, but it isn't always as calm as the composer's dreamy sea-piece suggests. Take waterproofs and be prepared for a fairly bumpy ride – you're crossing the Atlantic, after all.

④ Turn inland, back up the valley to its head. Pass the low walls of two ruined cottages and continue in the same direction for about 200yds (183m) to a fence corner. Keep the fence on your left, picking a way through heather, rock and bog on sheep paths. Dun I with its cairn appears ahead – aim directly for it to reach the edge of fields, where a fence runs across ahead. Turn right along it to a small iron gate.

> **WHAT TO LOOK FOR** ℹ
> The shingle at Coracle Bay has **cairns** (stone memorials) originally built by penitential monks. Over the years they have been renewed by visitors. Here you'll find greenish-white lumps of **Iona marble** among the grey gneiss. A long mound in the grass above the beach is supposed to indicate the dimensions of Columba's boat – 100ft (30m) long.

> **WHERE TO EAT AND DRINK** ℹ
> On the island, you can try the **Martyr's Bay Restaurant** which offers fresh local seafood (March–November; dogs on the patio only). For a quick snack there's the **Heritage Tea Room** with its garden at the abbey.

⑤ This leads to a track that passes **Ruanaich farm** to the tarred road of the outward walk. Cross into a farm track, which bends to the right at **Maol**. It reaches **Baile Mor** (the Iona village) at the ruined nunnery. Just ahead is the abbey with its squat square tower, or turn right directly to the ferry pier.

Walk 3

Climbing to the Castle of Cups

Dun na Cuaiche offers a fine view of Inveraray, the Campbell capital of Argyll.

•DISTANCE•	4 miles (6.4km)
•MINIMUM TIME•	2hrs 15min
•ASCENT / GRADIENT•	900ft (274m) ▲▲▲
•LEVEL OF DIFFICULTY•	👫 👫 👫
•PATHS•	Clear, mostly waymarked paths, no stiles
•LANDSCAPE•	Steep, wooded hill, some rocky outcrops
•SUGGESTED MAP•	aqua3 OS Explorer 363 Cowal East
•START / FINISH•	Grid reference: NN 096085
•DOG FRIENDLINESS•	Must be under control, not necessarily on lead
•PARKING•	Pay-and-display, Inveraray Pier
•PUBLIC TOILETS•	Inveraray Pier and Castle

BACKGROUND TO THE WALK

Inveraray is the seat of the Duke of Argyll, chieftain of Clan Campbell. Thus it became, in the eyes of Campbells anyway, the capital of the southern Highlands.

The Campbells Have Come

Until about 1600, the main power in the Highlands was MacDonald, Lord of the Isles. The Duke of Argyll aimed to take his place – by the normal methods of intrigue and armed attack on neighbouring clans, but also by collaboration with the legal government in Edinburgh and the King in London. Clan Campbell would hit you with fire and the sword, but also with a writ from the Privy Council. As a result they became the most powerful and the most universally disliked of all the clans.

In 1691, King William demanded an oath of loyalty from the rebellious Highland chieftains. MacIan of the Glen Coe MacDonalds was required to sign his oath in Inveraray. He hesitated over this visit to the capital of his hated rivals, and eventually arrived two days after the deadline. His delay was made the pretext for the Campbell-led Massacre of Glen Coe (► Walk 11). When a Campbell was murdered in Appin 60 years later, the suspect, James Stewart of the Glens, was tried at Inveraray before a jury of Campbells, with Argyll himself as judge. The hanging of Stewart, who was almost certainly innocent, is still resented in the MacDonald country.

Argyll Rebuilds

With the breaking of the clan system in 1745, Argyll felt confident enough to pull down his fortified castle and rebuild in a style that suited a wealthy landowner who no longer needed to resort to violence to control his lands.

The present building, greatly admired by Sir Walter Scott, is described as a country house in the style of a castle. Its grey stone, quarried from just above the town, is sombre, but tones well with the muted green and blue of the Campbell tartan. To go with his new castle, Argyll decided he needed a new town. Some say that old Inveraray was simply too close to the castle. But in its present position, curved around its bay, it's a magnificent and early example of a modern, planned town. It is dominated by the Court House where James of the Glens stood his trial, and by the white arches of the Argyll Hotel. One of these arches supplies a surprising passageway for the today's A819.

The Duke of Argyll completed his ambitious rebuilding scheme with avenues and bridges; one of the bridges forms an elegant entry to the town on the A83. This walk crosses the Garden Bridge, designed by John Adam (1721–92) of the famous Scottish family of architects. The whole layout of castle and town is splendidly seen from the summit of Dun na Cuaiche (Castle of Cups).

Walk 3 Directions

① Follow the seafront past the Argyll Hotel and bear left towards **Inveraray Castle**. At the first junction, turn right past a football pitch with a standing stone. After the coach park on the left and the end wall of the castle on the right, the estate road on the left is signed 'Dun na Cuaiche Walk'. It passes a memorial to clansmen who were killed for religious reasons in 1685. Cross the stone-arched **Garden Bridge** to a junction.

② Turn right to a riverside track and follow it to a picnic table with a view back to the castle. A rough track runs up left, but turn off instead on to a small path just to right of this, beside a stone gatepost. It climbs quite steeply through an area where attempts are currently being made to eradicate rhododendron (but the roddies are winning).

WHILE YOU'RE THERE ⓘ

Inveraray Castle is open to visitors from April to mid-October. Its interiors are even more spectacular and decorated than the outside. Disused weapons – 1,100 muskets and axes – have been formed into fantastic ornaments for the Armoury Hall.

---

③ At a green track above, turn left, slightly downhill, for 50yds (46m). Steps on the right lead up to a terraced path that goes slightly downhill around the hillside for ¼ mile (400m). Turn sharp right up a steep path with a rope handrail. This works its way back around the hill, passing below a small crag. Where it crosses a couple of open screes, there are fine views out to the right over Inveraray. At a path junction, turn left, following a waymarker pole up through woods. As the slope eases, the path crosses a grassy clearing to meet a wider one. Turn left, in zig-zags, to reach the summit of **Dun na Cuaiche**. The tower at the top is placed so it can be seen from below, but also offers outstanding views.

WHERE TO EAT AND DRINK ⓘ

The **Poacher** licensed restaurant on Inveraray Pier is a cheerful tea shop specialising in good coffee, salmon and other 'Fyne' foods. They'll try and persuade you to sample Irn-bru, Scotland's soft drink reputedly made from sugar and iron girders. About 90 per cent of visitors agree it's quite nice. There's another tea room at the castle.

---

④ Return down the path to the clearing, but this time keep ahead. The path, rather muddy, bends left then enters the plantation and becomes a clear track. It passes between two dry-stone pillars where a wall crosses, turns back sharp left, and passes between two more pillars lower down the same wall. Continue down the track, ignoring side-tracks on the left, to a **lime kiln** on the right.

⑤ Below the lime kiln, a gate leads out into an open field. Cross this diagonally left, going straight over a track to a kissing gate beyond. This leads into a wood of sycamores, and bluebells if you're here in May. The path runs down to the track junction before the **Garden Bridge** (Point ②). Return along the castle driveway to **Inveraray**.

WHAT TO LOOK FOR ⓘ

The surroundings are sprinkled with decorative **small buildings**. The tower on Dun na Cuaiche was built 'in the style of a ruin' by William Adam, father of John. He also designed the white-painted cylindrical dovecote seen from Garden Bridge. On Walk 4 you'll pass a hexagonal summer house built for viewing the waterfall on the River Aray, and the 'rusticated grotto' at Bealach an Fhuarain. This was also designed by William Adam and covers the spring that supplies water to Inveraray.

River Aray and Coille-bhraghad Wood

The Queen's Drive, the Duke's ornamental well and the town of Inveraray.
See map and information panel for Walk 3

•DISTANCE•	6¾ miles (10.9km)
•MINIMUM TIME•	3hrs
•ASCENT / GRADIENT•	500ft (152m) ▲▲ ▲ ▲
•LEVEL OF DIFFICULTY•	👣👣 👣 👣

Walk 4 Directions
(Walk 3 option)

Follow Walk 3 to Point ②, the **Garden Bridge**. Bear slightly right on a path into woodland with a blue waymarker. Where it ends at a kissing gate, turn left on a track, which joins a tarred estate road. Keep ahead along this, to pass the white-painted **dovecote**, and reach **Carloonan farm** (Point Ⓐ). Pass between the buildings to join a track emerging from the farm.

After 300yds (274m) this reaches **Carloonan Bridge**. Turn left across this, and left again on a track alongside the river. Just before the edge of the trees, turn right to reach the **A819** (Point Ⓑ).

Cross to the old road beyond and turn right, then left on an old track with a stream on its left. At a well-used track, turn left across the stream. Where a left fork leads back to the **A819**, bear right instead, and right again on to a wide, gently climbing forest road. This is the **Queen's Drive**, used by Queen Victoria on a visit to a vanished waterfall. At the top of the road, a bench on the left (Point Ⓒ) gives views to the Arrochar Hills, including the Cobbler.

After another short climb, bear left on the main track to a stone bridge (Point Ⓓ). Upstream was the waterfall Queen Victoria visited: the creation of a reservoir further up has removed its water.

The main track continues past a fish pond on the left and a **ruin** on the right, then climbs to a junction. Keep ahead on a smaller track downhill. This descends into a valley under tall Douglas firs. At the foot of the glen (Point Ⓔ), the track on the left passes a **waterworks** and runs along the foot of the wood. After ½ mile (800m), bear left up a track to the little classical **temple**, a wellhead built by William Adam in 1747 (Point Ⓕ).

Continue downhill; turn right along the foot of the wood almost to the previous junction. A kissing gate on the left leads out of the wood and across a track into **Newtown**. At the foot of the street turn left on to a track through a car park. The **Bell Tower** is on the left; opposite, a gap leads to **Inveraray Jail**. Turn left along the main street to the pier.

Walk 5

The Shores of Loch Scridain

A walk through Mull's basalt landscape to the ancient fort of Dun Bhuirg.

•DISTANCE•	8¼ miles (13.3km)
•MINIMUM TIME•	4hrs 15min
•ASCENT / GRADIENT•	1,200ft (365m) ▲▲ ▲
•LEVEL OF DIFFICULTY•	🚶🚶 🚶 🚶
•PATHS•	Track and short path, 1 stile
•LANDSCAPE•	Windswept hillsides above loch
•SUGGESTED MAP•	aqua3 OS Explorer 373 Iona, Staffa & Ross of Mull or
	375 Isle of Mull East
•START / FINISH•	Grid reference: NM 477275
•DOG FRIENDLINESS•	On lead near livestock
•PARKING•	½ mile (800m) beyond Tiroran farm
•PUBLIC TOILETS•	None on route
•NOTE•	Can extend walk to fossil tree – much tougher with extra
	3¼ miles (5.3km)

Walk 5 Directions

To reach the walk start, turn off the **B8035** at **Kilfinichen Bay**, following a blue sign for Burg. The road passes just below the high-tide mark and, after **Tiroran farm**, becomes a rough track.

From the car park, the track leads into a wood of rhododendron, pine and larch, then climbs gently. Ignore a branch down to the left (to Scobuil), but fork right, climbing rather steeply to open heather moor. You may see deer here. On the opposite side of Loch Scridain, and ahead on the Ardmeanach peninsula, is a lava landscape; lava flows have created a layered effect. Basalt lava is rich in minerals and the land between the crags is green and fertile. The track descends in bends and runs forward towards **Tavool House**. This was formerly a YMCA property but is now run by the Roses Project in Oban for the benefit of disadvantaged young people from the English Midlands.

Just before Tavool, fork down left on a fainter track with a sign, 'Fossil Tree'. The track descends into a steeply wooded valley, crossing two streams, one with a small waterfall. The rock here is black basalt, stained orange in places. The orange colour represents the top surfaces of the flow, weathered by the tropical climate of 60 million years ago. At a gate with a stile, the track enters National Trust for Scotland (NTS) land. **Burg Farm** was one of the Trust's first properties, bequeathed in 1932. Just before the farm, bear left on a rough track signed 'footpath'. A small shed is on the right and, on the left, a knoll with two cairns, commemorating Duncan and Christina MacGillivray, better known by the surname Burg, from the farm. Burg is still referred to locally as Chrissie's Cottage.

After ½ mile (800m) is **Dun Bhuirg**, a second knoll on the left, with a cairn. Lichen has made the granite inscription hard to read on dull days. It commemorates a lass called Daisy and her favourite place, which she called 'Castle Dare'.

> **WHERE TO EAT AND DRINK** ⓘ
> **Kinloch Hotel** is at the head of Loch Scridain, opposite an old drove road that crosses the bay through the waters of the River Coladair at low tide. Two posts mark the line of the ford. The hotel has a restaurant, and serves bar meals with a view of Ben More (children and dogs welcome; open Easter to mid-October).

About 50yds (46m) above the dun, a crag overhang offers shelter and a fine view and, just to the left, is a cave, suitable only for sheep. A gap between the cave and the overhang leads through to a little rock den. The path continues past the dun, descending gently for ¼ mile (400m) to the sea.

If you are feeling energetic, you can extend the walk at this point. From the shoreline just beyond Dun Bhuirg, the way to the **fossil tree** continues past a stone enclosure and along level grassy ground. At the first headland, the ground steepens and the path becomes clear again, slanting very gradually up the slope above the sea, with a line of basalt crag above.

The path arrives on a bouldery shelf, with a high steep slope above that leads to more crags. Below on the shoreline are some striking basalt formations. Soon you will see one of the two waterfalls that cascade on to the beach ahead. The clear path now turns sharply down left in a shallow gully and, after 20yds (18m), reaches the top of an

iron ladder. (The section leading down to the ladder is steep, and requires care, especially when wet.) The ladder's 25 steps lead down to the shore. Continue along the shoreline, passing below the two waterfalls on slippery boulders. From the second waterfall, go round into the next small bay (just 100yds/91m further). The **fossil tree** has a cave to its right, a large boulder on the shore just below and a small area of columnar basalt on its left. The cast of the tree is a hollow half-cylinder about 4ft (1.2m) wide, starting just above ground level. Return to **Dun Bhuirg** by the same route.

Turn back sharply left along the shore. The way is grassy at first, then rougher with some boulders and bog as it passes below the dun. Ahead is a small bay of black sand. As you cross this you may notice in the basalt shoreline slab some older boulders overwhelmed by the lava flow of 60 million years ago.

Just behind the bay are two ancient cairns, almost lost under bracken. Cross a grassy meadow and slant up through a gap in a fallen wall. Just above is the track, marked by telephone poles. Rejoin it and retrace the outward journey past **Tavool** to the car park.

> **WHILE YOU'RE THERE** ⓘ
> **Torosay Castle** is more of a Victorian mansion than a castle. Its grounds include rhododendrons, a woodland garden and a bog garden. The castle is linked to Craignure ferry terminal by a 2-mile (3.2km) narrow-gauge railway line. The castle and railway are open from Easter to October, the gardens year-round. You might see golden eagles on this remote coastline, and possibly an otter down along the shoreline.

Walk 6

The Black Wood of Rannoch

Looking between the branches of the ancient Caledonian forest to Loch Rannoch and Ben Alder.

•DISTANCE•	3¾ miles (6km)
•MINIMUM TIME•	2hrs 30min
•ASCENT / GRADIENT•	1,150ft (350m) ▲▲▲
•LEVEL OF DIFFICULTY•	🚶🚶 🚶🚶 🚶🚶
•PATHS•	Forest roads, rough woodland paths, no stiles
•LANDSCAPE•	Birch wood, plantations, ancient pine forest
•SUGGESTED MAP•	aqua3 OS Explorer 385 Rannoch Moor & Ben Alder
•START / FINISH•	Grid reference: NN 590567
•DOG FRIENDLINESS•	Off lead in woodland, but at heel in Black Wood
•PARKING•	Small pull-in just west of Rannoch School
•PUBLIC TOILETS•	Carie (forest car park), 2 miles (3.2km) east

BACKGROUND TO THE WALK

The Black Wood of Rannoch gets its sombre name simply because it consists of pines, rather than more colourful birch or oak. None of its trees has been planted by humans; surrounded by spruce plantations, and damaged by grazing deer, it still represents a remnant of the ancient Caledonian forest.

The Great Wood of Caledon

As the ice retreated during the last ice age, the trees moved in. Once the climate had stabilised, Scotland was one forest almost to the mountain tops. In the warmer west, the tree-cover consisted of oak (► Walk 16); in the north eastern valleys it was the birch. But the slopes of the Grampians were clothed in magnificent Scots pine.

A warm wet spell after the ice age, with the build-up of soggy inhospitable peat, contributed to the decline of the pine. But their main enemy has been humans. Forest that once stretched from Rannoch to Inverness was destroyed piece by piece for various reasons. In the 14th century, the Wolf of Badenoch (the brother of King Robert the Bruce) roamed and plundered this country, burning large areas of forest because they made it easier for his enemies to escape. In the 1500s, Queen Elizabeth of England prohibited iron smelting in parts of her kingdom, which drove the fuel-hungry smelters north into the Highlands. A hundred years later, forests were being destroyed around Rannoch to prevent their giving shelter to Macgregors, wolves and other undesirables.

Nibbled to Death

After the Jacobite rebellions, English timber companies moved in, and as clan chieftains became absentee landlords, they too needed timber cash to support their lavish new lifestyles. The felling of ancient pines continued through the two world wars.

The coming of sheep meant that where ancient forest still stood, any seedlings would be nibbled to death. However, two centuries of non-regeneration aren't enough to extinguish a pine wood. Today such remnants are being fenced and protected, and are coming alive again with new growth.

Proper Forest and Granny Pines

As you reach Point ④ of this walk, your spirits should suddenly rise. You have passed from what the Forestry Commission calls a forest, where trees destined to become pulp for paper stand trunk to trunk in grey gloom, to emerge under a more open canopy, where views are wide and where sunlight reaches the pine-needle floor and brightens the undercover of bilberry and heather. The cheerful reddish bark complements the dark green of the foliage above.

Here and there you will come across an old pine that is too twisted or distorted to be of any use in shipbuilding, which has been allowed to live on through the centuries – a so-called granny pine. The lifespan of a pine is 300 years or more, so these trees will have seen the last of the wolves pass by, and sheltered broken men after Bonnie Prince Charlie's failed rebellion in 1746.

Walk 6 Directions

① From the pull-in, walk back along the road with **Loch Rannoch** on your left and **Rannoch School** on the right. You pass its commando climbing tower on the right, its sailing centre on the left and its golf course. At the school's goods entrance, a Scottish Rights of Way Society (SRWS) signpost

Walk 6

WHILE YOU'RE THERE ⓘ
The first exploiters of the Caledonian forest were the Caledonians themselves: Iron-Age Celts of 2,500 years ago. A unique insight into their lives can be found at the **Scottish Crannog Centre** at Kenmore, beside Loch Tay. Here you can walk through a reconstructed lake village built on pinewood stilts driven into the loch which shows what life was like thousands of years ago.

points up to the right – this is an old and unused through route to Glen Lyon. Follow the tarred driveway past tennis courts to the first buildings and turn left at another SRWS signpost.

② A sketchy path runs up under some fine birch trees. At an empty gateway in a decomposing fence it enters larch trees and becomes a narrow track that's a little damp in places. Avoid a lesser path turning off to the left; the main one becomes a pleasant green path contouring across the slope with glimpses of Loch Rannoch on the right. The path runs up to a wide forest road.

③ Ignore the path continuing opposite and turn right, contouring around the hill. Clear-felling has opened up views to Loch Rannoch

WHAT TO LOOK FOR ⓘ
A low, star-like flower below the birches at the walk's start could be mistaken for the common wood anemone, but is actually **chickweed wintergreen**. It can be identified by the rosette of leaves half-way up the flower stem. Most flowering plants die back in autumn to allow them to escape the frosts and winds, but on the sheltered forest floor, evolution has programmed this plant to keep its leaves through the winter – hence the name.

and the remote hills beyond. The highest of these, with a steep right edge, is Ben Alder, the centre of the southern Highlands. This hill is glimpsed from many places, notably the A9 at Dalwhinnie, but isn't easily reached from anywhere. After ½ mile (800m), keep ahead where another track joins from the left. The joined tracks descend to a triangle junction. Turn left, gently uphill and, after 220yds (201m), bear right on to a little-used old track. This descends to a bridge over the **Dall Burn**.

WHERE TO EAT AND DRINK ⓘ
From the head of Loch Rannoch, the former 'Road to the Isles' runs on for 5 miles (8km) to **Rannoch Station**. The great moor featured briefly in the film *Trainspotting* (1996), perhaps to show that the countryside can be as bleak as any run-down corner of Edinburgh. The austere impression is rather spoilt by the warm and friendly little café in the listed Swiss chalet-style station building. It's open from March to October and welcomes dogs.

④ Some 120yds (110m) after the bridge, the track bends left; here a path descends on the right. This is the **Black Wood of Rannoch**, now a forest reserve. The path runs under beautiful pines and birches. On the right, the Dall Burn is sometimes in sight and can always be heard. The path is quite rough, but unmistakable as it cuts through deep bilberry and heather. After a mile (1.6km), the path bends left to a track. Turn right to leave the Caledonian Reserve at a notice board. At a T-junction, turn left, away from the bridge leading into **Rannoch School**. The track improves as it runs past the school's indoor swimming pool to the lochside road.

Blair Castle and Glen Tilt

Following Queen Victoria into the great through route of the Grampians.

•DISTANCE•	6½ miles (10.4km)
•MINIMUM TIME•	3hrs 15min
•ASCENT / GRADIENT•	852ft (250m) ▲▲▲
•LEVEL OF DIFFICULTY•	👟 👟 👟
•PATHS•	Estate tracks and smooth paths, 1 stile
•LANDSCAPE•	Castle grounds, woodland, wild river valley and mountains
•SUGGESTED MAP•	aqua3 OS Explorers 386 Pitlochry & Loch Tummel; 394 Atholl
•START / FINISH•	Grid reference: NN 866662 (on Explorer 386)
•DOG FRIENDLINESS•	On leads on open grazing land
•PARKING•	Castle main car park
•PUBLIC TOILETS•	Opposite driveway to castle
•NOTE•	Track through firing range closed on a few days each year (mostly weekdays). Consult Atholl Estate Ranger service

BACKGROUND TO THE WALK

Since humans first arrived, Tilt has been a natural highway. King Robert the Bruce marched down Glen Tilt in 1306 on his way to a minor defeat near Tyndrum. Some 200 years later James V and Mary, Queen of Scots attended a deer drive in 1529, but the next monarch to complete the whole route was Queen Victoria. She came this way with Prince Albert on the third of their 'great expeditions' from Balmoral. Along with the Christmas tree and the 'Scottish Baronial' style of architecture, multi-day hill walks were ideas introduced from Thuringia in Germany by the Prince Consort. Today we'd call it backpacking, except that the packs were carried by ponies and so were the people for much of the way. Even so, 69 miles (111km) from Dalwhinnie to Balmoral in a day was a considerable trek. Two bagpipers forded the Tarff side-stream waist deep, playing all the time, while the Queen came behind on her pony, led by her special ghillie, John Brown.

An Angry Duke

Kings and cattle thieves, soldiers and shepherds have used Glen Tilt for thousands of years, and its right-of-way status is self-evident. But in 1840, the then Duke of Atholl, whose castle lay at its foot, felt he could make his own law. He did, after all, boast Britain's only private army. He tried to turn back a botanical expedition lead by a certain Professor Balfour. The professor won the right to walk the route, and his victory is commemorated in a ballad:

> 'There's ne'er a kilted chiel
> Shall drive us back this day, man.
> It's justice and it's public richt
> We'll pass Glen Tilt afore the nicht,
> For Dukes shall we care ae bawbee?
> The road's as free to you and me
> As to his Grace himself, man'

Responsible Access

Today a general right of responsible access to all hill ground is generally accepted, and about to be given the force of law by the Scottish Parliament. An 'Access Code', with the same status as the Highway Code for motorists, will define responsible access. During the deer-stalking season, from mid-August to October, polite and reasonable requests from the estate will be respected by hill walkers. Such a request is made at Gilbert's Bridge (▶ Point ④).

Walk 7 Directions

① Turn right in front of the castle to a four-way signpost, and bear right for a gate into **Diana's Grove**.

Bear left on a wide path to Diana herself. Turn right on a path that leads to a giant redwood tree, then bear left, to cross **Banvie Burn** on a footbridge alongside a road bridge. A gate leads to the road.

② You are now at **Old Blair**. Turn right and follow **Minigaig Street** uphill. It eventually becomes a track and enters forest. Ignore a track on the left and, in another ¼ mile (400m), fork right. In 60yds (55m) you pass a path down to the right with a green waymarker. This is the return route if the firing range ahead is closed. Otherwise keep ahead to emerge from the trees at the firing range gate.

WHERE TO EAT AND DRINK
At **Blair Atholl Water Mill and Tea Room** they don't just bake their own scones and shortbread, the flour and oatmeal are also ground on the premises. The mill dates from 1613, but the tea room is more recent; both are open from Easter to October (but not to dogs).

③ A red flag flies here if the range is in use, but read the notice carefully as on most firing days the track route through the range may be used. Follow the main track gently downhill, well below the firing range targets, until you get to the riverside, then fork right to reach **Gilbert's Bridge**.

④ Cross and turn right over a cattle grid. Follow the track for 220yds (201m), then turn left up a steep little path under trees to a stile.

WHILE YOU'RE THERE
White-painted **Blair Castle** dominates Glen Garry. It claims to be the most-visited historic house in Scotland, with Queen Victoria, Bonnie Prince Charlie and Robert the Bruce among its early guests. Under a fine set of turrets and battlements, it has 32 elegant apartments in styles covering five centuries. Blair was one of the first of Scotland's private houses to open its doors to the public.

WHAT TO LOOK FOR
After a visit to admire the nearby **Falls of Bruar** in 1787, the poet Robert Burns in his *Humble Petition of Bruar Water* appealed to the Duke of Atholl to plant more trees. The duke took the hint, with 27 million conifers going into the estate over a period of 50 years. **Diana's Grove** is named after the classical Roman goddess of hunting, whose statue stands among 100-year-old specimens of various exotic conifers. Recent measurements show that several are Britain's biggest of their species.

A green track now runs down-valley with fine views. It passes along the top of a mixed birchwood. Once through a gate into the wood, keep on the main track, gently uphill. After the gate out of the wood, there's a view across Blair Castle to Schiehallion. Another gate leads on to a gravel track and then a tarred road.

⑤ Turn right, down a long hill, crossing some waterfalls on the way down. At the foot of the hill turn right, signed 'Old Blair', to cross the **Old Bridge of Tilt**, then turn left into a car park.

⑥ Just to the right of a signboard, yellow waymarkers indicate a path that passes under trees to the **River Tilt**. Turn right through an exotic grotto until wooden steps on the right lead up to the corner of a caravan park. Head directly away from the river under pines. Ignore a track on the right and, at the corner of the caravan park, keep ahead under larch trees following a faint path. Cross a track to take the clear path ahead towards **Blair Castle**. Bear left at a statue of Hercules, passing the **Hercules Garden** (which you may walk round) to the front of the castle.

Walk 8

The Braes o' Killiecrankie

A deeply wooded riverside leads from the famous battlefield to Loch Faskally.

•DISTANCE•	8¾ miles (14.1km)
•MINIMUM TIME•	4hrs
•ASCENT / GRADIENT•	492ft (150m) ▲▲▲
•LEVEL OF DIFFICULTY•	👣👣 👣👣 👣👣
•PATHS•	Wide riverside paths, minor road, no stiles
•LANDSCAPE•	Oakwoods on banks of two rivers
•SUGGESTED MAP•	aqua3 OS Explorer 386 Pitlochry & Loch Tummel
•START / FINISH•	Grid reference: NN 917626
•DOG FRIENDLINESS•	Off leads on riverside paths
•PARKING•	Killiecrankie visitor centre
•PUBLIC TOILETS•	At start

BACKGROUND TO THE WALK

> *'If ye'd hae been where I hae been*
> *Ye wouldna been sae swanky o*
> *If ye'd hae seen where I hae seen*
> *On the braes o Killiecrankie o'*

The song commemorating the victory of the Battle of Killiecrankie in July 1689 is still sung wherever anyone with an accordion sits down in a pub full of patriotic tourists. In fact, both sides in the battle were Scots. When James II was ousted from England in a bloodless coup in 1688, the Scots Parliament (the Estates) voted to replace him with William of Orange. The Stuarts had neglected and mismanaged Scotland, and had mounted a bloody persecution of the fundamentalist Protestants (Covenanters) of the Southern Uplands.

'Bluidy Clavers'

John Claverhouse, 'Bonnie Dundee', had earned the rather different nickname 'Bluidy Clavers' in those persecutions. He now raised a small army of Highlanders in support of King James. The Estates sent a larger army north under another Highlander, General Hugh Mackay, to sort things out. Dundee, outnumbered two to one, was urged to ambush Mackay in the Pass of Killiecrankie. He refused, on the grounds of chivalry. The path above the river was steep, muddy and wide enough for only two soldiers; a surprise attack on such difficult ground would give his broadsword-wielding Highlanders too great an advantage against Mackay's inexperienced troops. Just one of the Lowlanders was picked off by an Atholl sharpshooter at the Trouper's Den (below today's visitor centre), and the battle actually took place on open ground, to the north of the pass.

Claymore Victorious

Killiecrankie was the last time the claymore conquered the musket in open battle, and it was down to a deficiency in the musket. Some 900 of the 2,500 Highlanders were shot down as they charged, but then the troopers had to stop to fix their bayonets, which plugged into the muzzle of the musket. By this time the Highlanders were upon them, and they broke and fled. The battle had lasted just three minutes. Half of Mackay's army was killed, wounded, captured or drowned in the Garry. One escaped by leaping 18ft (5.5m) across the river; the 'Soldier's Leap' is near the start of the walk. But the victory led nowhere. Bonnie Dundee died in the battle. A month later his army was defeated at Dunkeld, and 25 years later, when the Highlanders next brought their broadswords south for the Stuarts, the troopers had learnt to fix a bayonet to the side of a musket where it no longer blocked the barrel.

Walk 8

Walk 8 Directions

① Cross the front of the visitor centre to steps, signed 'Soldier's Leap', leading down into the wooded gorge. A footbridge crosses the waterfall of **Troopers' Den**. At the next junction, turn left ('Soldier's Leap'). Ten steps down, a spur path on the right leads to the viewpoint above the **Soldier's Leap**.

Walk 8

② Return to the main path, signed 'Linn of Tummel', which runs down to join the **River Garry** below the railway viaduct. After a mile (1.6km) it reaches a footbridge.

WHILE YOU'RE THERE

At the Pitlochry dam that forms Loch Faskally, Scottish and Southern Energy has a small **visitor centre** celebrating its hydro-electric schemes. It also has a window into the salmon ladder beside the dam. From March to October you can watch the fish battle their way up towards Killiecrankie.

③ Don't cross this footbridge, but continue ahead, signed 'Pitlochry', along the riverside under the tall South Garry road bridge. The path runs around a huge river pool to a tarred lane; turn right here. The lane leaves the lochside, then passes a track on the right, blocked by a vehicle barrier. Ignore this; shortly turn right at a signpost, 'Pitlochry'.

④ Immediately bear left to pass along the right-hand side of **Loch Dunmore**, following red-top posts. A footbridge crosses the loch, but turn away from it, half right, on to a small path that becomes a dirt track. After 110yds (100m) it reaches a wider track. Turn left, with a white/yellow waymarker. After 220yds (201m) the track starts to climb; here the white/yellow markers indicate a smaller path on the right, which follows the lochside. Where it rejoins the wider path, bear right at a green

waymarker and cross a footbridge to the **A9** road bridge.

⑤ Cross **Loch Faskally** on the Clunie footbridge below the road's bridge and turn right, on to a quiet road around the loch. In 1 mile (1.6km), at the top of the grass bank on the left, is the **Priest Stone**. After the **Clunie power station**, you reach a car park on the left. Here a sign indicates a steep little path down to the **Linn of Tummel**.

WHERE TO EAT AND DRINK

There are **cafés** at the start and at Lochside, Pitlochry. Pitlochry itself is the town of the tea room. One of them is **Macdonald's**, on the main street. You can get good bar meals at the **Old Mill Inn**, which also offers 100 malt whiskies and a waterwheel (children welcome; dogs in the outside seating area only).

⑥ Return to the road above for ½ mile (800m), to cross a grey suspension bridge on the right. Turn right, downstream, to pass above the **Linn**. A spur path back right returns to the falls at a lower level, but the main path continues along the riverside (signed 'Killiecrankie'). It bends left and goes down wooden steps to the **Garry**, then runs upstream and under the high road bridge. Take the side-path up on to the bridge for the view of the river, then return to follow the descending path signed 'Pitlochry via Faskally'. This runs down to the bridge, Point ③. Return upstream to the start.

WHAT TO LOOK FOR

Between the two world wars, much of the southern Highlands was developed with small scale hydro-electric schemes. Loch Faskally is artificial, and you'll pass the **Clunie power station**. Its stone arch commemorates the five people who died in the construction of the Clunie Tunnel, which brings water from Loch Tummel. Small hydro schemes do less damage than most forms of energy generation, but there is a price to pay: the Linn of Tummel was the Tummel Falls until it was half-drowned by Loch Faskally.

Slopes of Ben Vrackie

High above Glen Garry for an eagle's-eye view of Blair Castle and Pitlochry.
See map and information panel for Walk 8

•**DISTANCE**•	9½ miles (15.3km)
•**MINIMUM TIME**•	5hrs
•**ASCENT / GRADIENT**•	1,575ft (480m) ▲▲▲
•**LEVEL OF DIFFICULTY**•	🚶🚶 🚶🚶 🚶

Walk 9 Directions
(Walk 8 option)

Don't cross the Clunie footbridge over **Loch Faskally** (Point ⑤), but keep ahead under the road bridge to the **Lochside Café**. Take its access road up to the **A924** and follow this main road across the railway and into **Pitlochry**. At the start of the 30mph limit is the corner of **Larchwood Road** (Point Ⓐ).

Sunnybank Cottage, on this corner, is where a local man, John Stewart, stabbed his cousin Donald. He stayed in the area in order to spy on the funeral in the belief that if he could manage to see light under his cousin's coffin as it passed on its way to the funeral he would get away with the killing. He emigrated, and though he returned later, was never charged with the crime.

Turn left up **Larchwood Road**. It climbs with a dog-leg to left and right, then bends right beside a pool. After the golf course, you reach a T-junction at **Moulin** village (Point Ⓑ). A standing stone called the **Dane Stone** is in a field on the left. Turn left here, signed 'Ben-y-Vrackie', and go up the lane into a car park on the right (Point Ⓒ).

A path leads up the **Moulin Burn**. Where a track crosses, turn right for a few steps, then continue uphill with the stream on your left. The path joins a higher track, then turns off on the right to a footbridge. Follow the stream up to the top of the woodland, where a gate (Point Ⓓ) leads on to open moor.

A path continues up to the right of the stream, then bends right to a bench with a fine view down **Glen Garry**. On joining a new stream, bear left on a smaller path signed 'Bealach Walk'. (The main path ahead leads, after a stiff climb, to the summit of Ben Vrackie.) After a stile and a waymark just above, the path becomes indistinct. It runs directly uphill, to pass just to the right of the obvious little pass (Point Ⓔ) just above.

Now the path becomes a clear track through the pass leading downhill. A sign points towards Killiecrankie. The track fords a stream, with a footbridge alongside. After two gates, turn left at a T-junction (Point Ⓕ) to continue downhill. Where the track reaches a tarred road, turn right, again signed for Killiecrankie. The road passes under the new **A9** to meet the older **B8079** opposite the visitor centre at the start of Walk 8.

Walk 10

Around Kinloch Rannoch

A wander round field paths, riversides and through a craggy wood.

•DISTANCE•	2¼ miles (3.6km)
•MINIMUM TIME•	1hr
•ASCENT / GRADIENT•	100ft (30m) ▲▲▲
•LEVEL OF DIFFICULTY•	👫 👫 👫
•PATHS•	Small but well-formed paths, sometimes muddy, 1 stile
•LANDSCAPE•	Oakwoods, large river, very large loch
•SUGGESTED MAP•	aqua3 OS Explorer 386 Pitlochry & Loch Tummel
•START / FINISH•	Grid reference: NN 661586
•DOG FRIENDLINESS•	Good, but care on short stretch of B846 without pavement
•PARKING•	Street parking in main square of Kinloch Rannoch
•PUBLIC TOILETS•	At start

Walk 10 Directions

From the north end of the bridge over the **River Tummel**, walk up the right-hand side of the square, past the post office. Turn right before the police station towards **Kinloch Rannoch Primary School**. Before the school, a sign, 'Riverside Path', points to the right. The tarred path has a small stream on its left. When it reaches the Tummel, it turns left to cross the stream by a footbridge.

The path continues alongside the River Tummel. Where it bends left into a housing estate, a small sign, 'Riverside Path', marks the smaller, earth path ahead. It passes through woodland close to the river, to emerge at a roadside car park with picnic tables.

Further along the road, a high gate on the opposite side is signed 'Hillside Path'. Follow the stony track uphill, then turn sharp left on to an earth track. This climbs gently through oak and beech woods, with the main road not far below.

The cliffs of **Craig Varr** are just above. A glacier that came down out of Rannoch Moor dug the bed of Loch Rannoch as it hit more level ground. It also chopped off the end of this hill spur to give Craig Varr its steep southern slope. Large boulders, cracked off by frost, have rolled down into the wood, with one huge split rock right beside the track. Its mossy condition shows that the rockfall took place many centuries ago, probably during the tail-end of the ice age. Smaller stones, dislodged in the same way, form scree above the wood.

WHAT TO LOOK FOR

The **peregrine falcon** nests on the crags of Craig Varr. It's shaped like a grouse, and with a similar rapid-flapping style of flight. When disturbed, it flies out from the hillside and rapidly reaches the other side of the valley. It hunts birds as big as pigeons by stooping from above, diving at speeds of up to 200mph (320kph). Peregrines suffered from pesticide residues, which they absorbed second-hand from their prey. After the banning of the most harmful chemicals, their numbers are now increasing.

The track passes through a gate with a stile alongside. In 150yds (137m) it bends uphill, past a waymarker; fork left here on a smaller path. This descends to a gate and footbridge just above the road, which it joins at the entrance to **Kinloch Rannoch Outdoor Centre** on the edge of the village.

Continue along the road for a few steps, crossing the **Allt Mor**. If you wish to shorten this already short walk, the main square is just ahead, otherwise turn sharp right on a track with a public footpath sign for Loch Rannoch Hotel. A board with a path map is on the left.

> **WHILE YOU'RE THERE** ℹ
> The **Queen's View Visitor Centre** at the east end of Loch Tummel has one of the finest views in Scotland – along the loch, with its little wooded island, to Schiehallion. For those who like their scenery indoors, away from the rain and midges, there's an audio-visual display.

On the right is a small but striking waterfall. The strata of the schist are sloped at an angle of about 45 degrees, downwards to the right. The strands of the stream run down the strata, then across them forming a diamond pattern. Allt means stream, and Mor (sometimes Mhor, but pronounced Vore) means large. Look out for a small metal man fishing the pool below the waterfall.

After an abandoned wildlife garden on the left, the route passes through a gate with a kissing gate alongside, on to a stony track. In 20yds (18m), the uphill track is signed for Craig Varr. The top of the crag is a popular viewpoint, poised 600ft (182m) above the village with sight-lines along lochs Rannoch and Tummel, but the route bears left on a path signed 'Loch Rannoch'. A wall runs below on the left. On the right you pass a stone arch containing a spring of clear water that flows into a pottery tank.

> **WHERE TO EAT AND DRINK** ℹ
> Kinloch Rannoch's **Dunalastair Hotel** has a formal restaurant but serves no bar meals. My own preference is for the **Tummel Inn**, to the east, above Loch Tummel. It has real ales, good bar meals and a superb view out across its loch. Children are welcome, and dogs in the bar, but not the eating area.

A kissing gate leads to the roadside near the **Rannoch Hotel**. Turn left, towards the village. Take care here as there is no pavement; walk round bends on the outside so you can be seen by drivers. Just before **Kinloch Rannoch**, the road bends left at what is called **Drive Into Loch Corner**. For motorists emerging from the village, a tempting straight leads to an open gateway with the chilly waters of Rannoch just below.

Just inside the 30mph limit, at the start of the pavement, turn right at a sign 'Riverside Path'. A 'Please Shut the Gate' notice indicates the correct gate, where a rough track leads to picnic tables at the riverside, surrounded by yellow-flowering broom bushes. A tall concrete weir controls the water level of Loch Rannoch here.

The path leads downstream, through a gate patterned with the Saltire (St Andrew's Cross) of Scotland and under birch trees. Alongside, the wide river roils and swirls in an unnatural fashion, caused by its passage through the weir. After passing under the road bridge, turn left past the public toilets to the village square.

Into the Lost Valley

A rugged waterfall walk into the hidden hollow where the MacDonalds hid their stolen cows.

•DISTANCE•	2¾ miles (4.4km)
•MINIMUM TIME•	2hrs 15min
•ASCENT / GRADIENT•	1,050ft (320m) ▲▲▲
•LEVEL OF DIFFICULTY•	🚶 🚶 🚶
•PATHS•	Rugged and stony, stream to wade through, 1 stile
•LANDSCAPE•	Crags and mountains
•SUGGESTED MAP•	aqua3 OS Explorer 384 Glen Coe & Glen Etive
•START / FINISH•	Grid reference: NN 168569
•DOG FRIENDLINESS•	Dogs must be reasonably fit and agile
•PARKING•	Lower of two roadside parking places opposite Gearr Aonach (middle one of Three Sisters)
•PUBLIC TOILETS•	Glencoe village

BACKGROUND TO THE WALK

The romantically named Lost Valley is 'Coire Gabhail' in Gaelic, the Corrie of Booty. Here, during the centuries leading up to the famous massacre of 1692, the MacDonalds hid their stolen cattle when the owners came storming in over the Moor of Rannoch with torch and claymore. It seems incredible that even the sure-footed black cattle of the clans could have been persuaded up the slope to Coire Gabhail. The corrie entrance is blocked by two old landslides from the face of Gearr Aonach, the middle hill of Glen Coe's Three Sisters. Stream shingle, backing up behind the obstruction, forms the smooth valley floor.

Noble Profession of Cattle Thief

The economic system of Highland Scotland, until the end of the clans in 1745, was based on the keeping and the stealing of cattle. It was an unsettled and dangerous lifestyle, and its artform was the verse of the bard who celebrated the most ingenious or violent acts of thievery and kept track of blood feuds.

Raiders of Glen Coe

The clan, gathered under its chieftain, was an organisation for protecting its own glen and for stealing from its neighbours. The MacDonalds of Glen Coe were particularly good at it. They raided right across the country, passing the fringes of the Cairngorms to steal from the fertile lands of Aberdeenshire and Moray. In 1689, when Campbell of Glen Lyon was a guest in the house of MacIan, chief of Glen Coe, his cold blue eyes may have dwelt on a particular cooking pot. Twice in the previous ten years, MacIan had come raiding into Glen Lyon, dishonoured the women by cutting off their hair and, on the second, occasion stolen that pot from Campbell's own mother.

The Massacre

By the late 1600s, the clan and the claymore were being replaced by a legal system backed by the central government and its army. But because they were so good at cattle thieving, the

MacDonalds of Glen Coe continued the practice long after everyone else had, reluctantly, started to move into the modern world of cash. As a result, the government decided to make an example of them.

On a cold February day, a squad of soldiers arrived in the valley. Traditional hospitality meant that even its leader Glen Lyon, a Campbell and an enemy, was welcomed into the house of MacDonald. Five nights later, at a given signal, the soldiers rose from their beds and started murdering their hosts. The Glen Coe Massacre was either incompetent or mercifully half-hearted. Of the valley's population of 300, just 40 were killed, with the remainder escaping through the snow to the Lost Valley and the other high corries.

Walk 11 **Directions**

① From the uphill corner of the car park, a faint path slants down to the old road, which is now a well-used track. Head up-valley for about 650yds (594m). With the old road continuing as a green track ahead,

your path now bends down to the right. It has been rebuilt, with the bog problem solved by scraping down to the bedrock. The path reaches the gorge where the **River Coe** runs in a geological dyke of softer rock. Descend on a steep wooden step ladder, to cross a spectacular footbridge.

② The ascent out of the gorge is on a bare rock staircase. Above, the path runs through regenerating birch wood, which can be very wet on the legs; sheep and deer have been excluded from the wood with a temporary fence. Emerge over this by a high ladder stile. The path, rebuilt in places, runs uphill for 60yds (55m). Here it bends left; an inconspicuous alternative path continues uphill, which can be used to bypass the narrow path of the main route.

③ The main route contours into the gorge of the **Allt Coire Gabhail**. It is narrow with steep drops below. Where there is an alternative of rock slabs and a narrow path just below, the slabs are more secure. You will hear waterfalls, then two fine ones come into view ahead. After passing these, continue between boulders to where the main path bends left to cross the stream below a boulder the size of a small house. (A small path runs on up to right of the stream, but leads nowhere useful.) The river here is wide and fairly shallow. Five or six stepping stones usually allow dry crossing. If the water is above the stones, then it's safer to wade alongside them; if the water is more than knee-deep the crossing should not be attempted.

④ A well-built path continues uphill, now with the stream on its right. After 100yds (91m) a lump of rock blocks the way. The path follows a slanting ramp up its right-hand side. It continues uphill, still rebuilt in places, passing above the boulder pile that blocks the valley, the result of two large rockfalls from under Gearr Aonach opposite. At the top of the rockpile the path levels, giving a good view into the **Lost Valley**.

⑤ Drop gently to the valley's gravel floor. The stream vanishes into the gravel, to reappear below the boulder pile on the other side. Note where the path arrives at the gravel, as it becomes invisible at that point. Wander up the valley to where the stream vanishes, ¼ mile (400m) ahead. Anywhere beyond this point is more serious hillwalking than you have done up to now on this walk. Return to the path and follow it back to the start of the walk.

Around the Small Shepherd

Two valley passes through the high mountains at the head of Glen Coe.

•DISTANCE•	8 miles (12.9km)
•MINIMUM TIME•	4hrs 30min
•ASCENT / GRADIENT•	1,300ft (396m) ▲▲▲
•LEVEL OF DIFFICULTY•	🏃 🏃 🏃
•PATHS•	Rough, unmade paths, some boggy bits, no stiles
•LANDSCAPE•	Remote high valleys into heart of hills
•SUGGESTED MAP•	aqua3 OS Explorer 384 Glen Coe & Glen Etive
•START / FINISH•	Grid reference: NN 213559
•DOG FRIENDLINESS•	Good, some streams to cross
•PARKING•	Large parking area on south side of A82, marked by yellow AA phone post
•PUBLIC TOILETS•	Glencoe village
•NOTE•	Fords in Lairig Eilde can be impassible or dangerous after heavy rain

BACKGROUND TO THE WALK

This walk uses two through routes on either side of Buachaille Etive Beag, the Small Herdsman of Etive. The Gaelic word 'Lairig' means a valley pass through the mountains. We use Lairig Gartain for the outward journey, and Lairig Eilde for the return, with a final link along the old Glen Coe road.

Passing Deer

This land is owned by the National Trust for Scotland, and there hasn't been any deer stalking for 65 years. When working on this book, I came across three hinds at the roadside car park. And one October I came through Lairig Eilde (Pass of the Deer) when its mountain walls were echoing with the roaring of the stags. It's an unforgettable sound – rather like a lion, but a little like a cow too.

For most of the year the hinds gather in small family groups with their calves of the last two years, while the stags go around in loose gangs. Deer dislike midges as much as humans do, so in summer they'll be on the high tops, though they may come down at night or in bad weather. In winter they'll be in the valley bottom or even at the roadside.

The calves are born in early June; they are dappled to camouflage them on the forest floor, which is their natural home. Within a few days they're running with the herd. The grace and speed of a week-old deer calf across a peat bog is the envy of any human hillwalker.

Getting into the Rut

The hinds have no antlers. The stags lose theirs in early summer and grow new ones ready for the rut: the September mating season. Large, many-branched antlers do not make a stag a better fighter, and are a serious drain on his system. They have probably evolved as display items, for intimidating other males and attracting females. A mighty roar may gain the stag the harem of a dozen hinds that he's after. If not, a quick clash of antlers will usually settle the matter. These displays are a way of determining which stag would have won without putting either to the risk of injury. However, the stag is sometimes prepared to fight for his wives and such fights can end in the death of one or even both males.

Kind to Be Cruel

Red deer owe their widespread survival in Scotland to the men who preserved and nurtured them in order to hunt them every autumn. For ancient aristocrats and newly rich Victorian manufacturers, the sport of sneaking up on a stag with a rifle was exciting, virile and also impressively expensive. With no predators, deer must still be culled by shooting, even on NTS land where no sport stalking takes place. Such culling will be done at dawn, before walkers start disturbing the hill.

Walk 12 Directions

① A signpost to Glen Etive, at the edge of the car park, marks the start of the path into **Lairig Gartain**. The path is clear, but very boggy in places. It heads up-valley with the **River Coupall** down on the left. Gradually it draws closer to the river, but does not cross it. A large cairn marks the top of the path, which is slightly to the right of the lowest point of the pass.

② The descending path is steeper, over boggy grass with a new stream forming on its left. After ½ mile (800m), a small path branches off left towards a waterfall below, but beware, as it's a wrong turning leading down to the roadside at Glen Etive, so stay on the main, higher path. This slants along the right-hand wall of the valley, getting ever higher above the stream. Eventually it emerges on to the steep south ridge of **Stob Dubh**.

> **WHILE YOU'RE THERE**
> The **Glencoe Folk Museum** occupies a heather-thatched house in the centre of the village. It has items of interest rather than value, such as china, toys and medical utensils from the Victorian age, and weapons that were hidden away after the Battle of Culloden.

> **WHAT TO LOOK FOR**
> The **lousewort** is a low plant with purple flowers, which slightly resembles heather but flowers earlier, in June and July. Its less common white variety outnumbers the pink on the way up Lairig Gartain. On the Etive side of the pass, only the pink form is seen. Once past the top of Lairig Eilde, almost all of the plants are white. This would indicate that the very tops of the two passes are barriers to this plant, allowing separate valley types to develop.

③ Here a path runs down to a gate in a deer fence, but there's no need to go any further downhill. Follow a faint path above the deer fence, descending to cross the **Allt Lairig Eilde**. If the stream is too full to cross, you can return and go down through the deer fence to a wider but shallower crossing, 200yds (183m) downstream. Alternatively, you can head up on a small path to right of the stream, hoping to find a safer crossing higher up. Having crossed the stream, follow the fence up to a gate at its corner. Turn up a wide path that rises out of **Glen Etive**.

④ The path ascends to the left of the stream, passing several waterfalls. Eventually it crosses the stream, now very much smaller, then continues straight ahead, crossing the col well to the right of its lowest point. A large cairn marks the top of the path.

⑤ The new, descending stream is also, confusingly, the **Allt Lairig Eilde**. The path crosses it by a wide, shallow ford and goes down its left bank. A mile (1.6km) further on, the path recrosses, using large boulders as stepping stones. It runs down to join the **A82** near the cairn that marks the entry into **Glen Coe**.

⑥ Cross the road, and the river beyond, to join the old Glencoe road at an arched culvert. Turn right along the firm track, which soon rejoins the new road, then cross diagonally, on to a damp path. This runs to the right of the new road, then recrosses. It soon rejoins the **A82** opposite the beginning of the walk.

> **WHERE TO EAT AND DRINK**
> The **Kingshouse Hotel** was built in 1590 as a hunting lodge for James VI (later James I of England). But its status as a 'king's house' dates from 1799, when a squad of redcoats was stationed there to protect travellers. Kingshouse was an overnight stop for the drovers bringing cattle south to market every autumn. The green flats, popular today as an informal camp ground, were overnight grazing. Today it's a much-appreciated stop-off for people on the West Highland Way, and for hillwalkers, climbers and skiers.

Walk 13

Grey Mare's Tail and Mamore Lodge

A waterfall, a shooting lodge and a ramble down the West Highland Way.

•DISTANCE•	3½ miles (5.7km)
•MINIMUM TIME•	2hrs 15min
•ASCENT / GRADIENT•	984ft (300m) ▲▲▲
•LEVEL OF DIFFICULTY•	🚶🚶 🚶🚶 🚶
•PATHS•	Well-made paths, one steep, rough ascent, no stiles
•LANDSCAPE•	Birchwoods leading to long views along Loch Leven
•SUGGESTED MAP•	aqua3 OS Explorer 384 Glen Coe & Glen Etive or 392 Ben Nevis & Fort William
•START / FINISH•	Grid reference: NN 187622
•DOG FRIENDLINESS•	Off lead unless sheep near by
•PARKING•	Grey Mare's Tail car park, Kinlochleven
•PUBLIC TOILETS•	Kinlochleven, at bridge over River Leven

BACKGROUND TO THE WALK

Aluminium is a very common metal: around eight per cent of the earth's crust is made up of it. It's very reactive, which means that it's extremely difficult to extract the aluminium atoms out of the ore called bauxite. There is no chemical method for this process. Instead, it's done by dissolving the ore in molten cryolite (a fluoride mineral) and applying vast quantities of electricity.

As a result, aluminium processing doesn't take place where you find the bauxite, but where you find the electricity, with lots of water coming down steep hillsides, and a deep-water harbour at the bottom, such as Kinlochleven.

The village of Kinlochleven was built around the smelter. Two lochs above have been dammed for hydro-electricity, and six huge pipes bring the water down from a control station above the Devil's Staircase footpath.

Pipeline or Path

A pipeline on the OS Landranger map is a dotted line, rather like a path. And it may be that the path of this walk happened by mistake, as walkers mistook the pipeline for a path, walked along it and so created the path that they thought was there in the first place. The pipeline path leads from the outflow of Loch Eilde Mor, around the head of Loch Leven along the 1,100ft (335m) contour, giving superb views towards the Pap of Glencoe and the loch's foot. Eventually, it carries Loch Eilde's water to the Blackwater Reservoir.

Why has the water from Loch Eilde been taken all the way round this hillside to the Blackwater Reservoir, instead of straight down to the turbines where it's actually needed? You need to glance across the valley at the six descending pipes for the answer. At the foot of those huge reinforced pipes the water is under 30 tons per square foot (300 tonnes/sq m) of pressure. A second such set from Loch Eilde would cost far more than the much longer, unpressurised pipe to the other reservoir. Besides, we wouldn't have ended up with this fine contour-line walk.

The Kinlochmore smelter started as one of the largest in the world, but by the end of the 1900s it was the world's smallest. It closed in 2000, although its turbines continue to generate electricity, which is now diverted to the smelter at Fort William or into the National Grid. The smelter had been the reason for Kinlochleven, and its main employer. Projects to keep Kinlochleven alive include the fine, newly constructed path system, the visitor centre and the Atlas Brewery on the site where carbon electrical connectors were once made.

Walk 13 **Directions**

① A smooth gravel path leads up out of the car park to multicoloured waymarks pointing left. The path

rises to a view through trees of the **Grey Mare's Tail** waterfall, then descends to a footbridge. Here turn left (blue waymarker) to visit the foot of the spectacular waterfall, then return to take the path on the

Walk 13

right (white, yellow and green waymarker). Follow the stream up for 100yds (91m), then turn left at a waymarker. The path, quite steep and loose, zig-zags up through birches to more open ground.

② Here the path forks. Take the right-hand branch, with a yellow and green waymarker, to pass under power lines. The path follows the crest of a heathery spur, then bends left to cross two streams. Immediately after the second stream is another junction.

WHILE YOU'RE THERE ⓘ
The **Aluminium Story Visitor Centre** at Kinlochleven is worth a quick visit, although its displays are entirely audio-visual. Alternatively, you could tour the **Atlas Brewery**, in a disused part of the aluminium works (after 5:30PM).

---

③ The confusing waymarker here has eight arrows in four colours. Turn left, following a white arrow slightly downhill, to cross a footbridge above a waterfall and red granite rocks. The path leads up under birches. Here the ground cover includes the aromatic bog myrtle, which can be used to discourage midges, though it is less effective than a chemical repellent. When the path reaches a track, turn left (white arrow). Below the track is a tin deer used by stalkers for target practice: it's more convenient than the real thing as it doesn't wander off just when you're creeping up on it. A signed footpath bypasses the **Keepers' Cottages** on the left, then rejoins the track beyond, to a junction above **Mamore Lodge**.

④ Keep ahead, above the lodge, climbing gently past two tin huts, self-catering accommodation

---

WHERE TO EAT AND DRINK ⓘ
The **Tailrace Inn**, in Kinlochleven, is a service station on the West Highland Way. They welcome children (if having a meal) and dogs (if well behaved). In summer, you won't get through an evening without a rousing chorus of *Bonnie Banks of Loch Lomond*. Try the Atlas Brewery's 'Wayfarer' ale, brewed for thirsty West Highland Way walkers.

---

labelled 'stable' and 'bothy'. At the high point of the track there is a TV mast on the right, a bench on the left and a view along Loch Leven ahead. The track descends gently, with slabs of whitish quartzite above. The wide path of the **West Highland Way** (WHW) can be seen below and gradually rises to join the track, with a large waymarker planted in a cairn.

⑤ Turn left down the West Highland Way path, which drops into the woods below. Watch out for a junction where the main path seems to double back to the right; take the smaller path, continuing ahead with a WHW waymarker. After crossing the tarred access track of **Mamore Lodge**, the path fords a small stream to reach the village. Turn left along the pavement and fork left into **Wades Road** to regain the car park.

WHAT TO LOOK FOR ⓘ
The view down the length of Loch Leven, which is such a feature of Walks 13 and 14, ends on the left with a small pointed mountain. Though only 2,434ft (742m) high, it's one of Scotland's sharpest peaks outside Skye. 'Sgurr na Ciche' describes its shape exactly: less explicit English translates it as the 'Pap' of Glencoe. Alan Breck and Davie Balfour sheltered high on its slopes in Robert Louis Stevenson's classic Highland novel *Kidnapped*.

Aluminium Landscape Above Kinlochleven

A sea loch, a mountain loch and a pipeline path above deep wooded glens.
See map and information panel for Walk 13

•DISTANCE•	6¾ miles (10.9km)
•MINIMUM TIME•	3hrs 45min
•ASCENT / GRADIENT•	1,400ft (426m) ▲▲▲
•LEVEL OF DIFFICULTY•	🚶🚶 🚶🚶 🚶

Walk 14 Directions (Walk 13 option)

Follow Walk 13 up to Point ③. At this junction turn right, following a yellow waymarker. The path climbs beside a stream, then bends right to cross it and another stream, to reach a track (Point Ⓐ). A continuation path rises briefly above the track then rejoins it.

Follow the track uphill towards a wide pass. Just before it, a path on the right is a short-cut back to Kinlochleven. At the pass (Point Ⓑ) is a view ahead along Loch Eilde Mor, the Big Loch of the Hind.

Descend for ¼ mile (400m) to a path forking off on the right. After 220yds (201m), bend right. A smaller path ahead goes only to the loch foot, while the main path leads to the right of a knoll to a dam over the **Allt na h-Eilde** (Point Ⓒ).

Turn right on to a rough and sometimes soggy track. This follows a concrete pipeline across the hill face, high above Kinlochleven, with fine views. In the pipeline below, look out for a rusty metal item like a tea-strainer on a stick – this is a pressure release valve. After 1¼ miles (2km), the path drops below the pipeline and, in another 200yds (183m), a cairn marks a steep path descending on the right (Point Ⓓ).

As you set off downhill, to the left you should see the Crowberry Tower on distant Buachaille Etive Mor, outlined against the sky. The path becomes very rough as it enters the wood, but then passes through a wall gap and rises slightly to join another path (Point Ⓔ). Bear right on this path to the edge of **Kinlochleven** (Point Ⓕ).

The track ahead has a West Highland Way marker. Shortly it becomes a street; look for the tarred path on the left where the WHW turns back to the riverside. You pass the tailrace at the former smelter to the road bridge (Point Ⓖ). You can turn up right into Kinlochleven here. For a longer walk, continue under the bridge to a riverside path. It bends right, past black garages, to an earth path upstream alongside the **Allt Coire na Ba**. A new path continues under hazels; where it ends, a few steps ahead you cross the **B863** into **Wade Road**. This leads to the car park.

Waterfalls and Wade's Walk

A sheltered forest ramble high above Loch Linnhe.

•DISTANCE•	2¾ miles (4.4km)
•MINIMUM TIME•	1hr 30min
•ASCENT / GRADIENT•	600ft (183m) ▲▲ ▲ ▲
•LEVEL OF DIFFICULTY•	林 林 林
•PATHS•	Well-made paths, forest tracks, no stiles
•LANDSCAPE•	Plantation and semi-wild forest
•SUGGESTED MAP•	aqua3 OS Explorer 384 Glen Coe & Glen Etive
•START / FINISH•	Grid reference: NN 029634
•DOG FRIENDLINESS•	Off lead in forest
•PARKING•	Forest Enterprise picnic place at road end, behind Inchree
•PUBLIC TOILETS•	Corran Ferry – bypass ferry queue and turn left into car park

Walk 15 Directions

At the bottom corner of the car park is a well-built path marked by a white waymarker. A field on its right gives views out across Loch Linnhe until it crosses a footbridge to enter woodland. The path runs gently uphill, through birchwoods with clearings of heather and grass. The **Inchree waterfalls** appear ahead, falling through a gorge lined with rhododendron.

There are seven waterfalls, though only the top three are visible from here. They are particularly fine after heavy rain, when spray drifts out above the treetops. The path turns uphill, staying about 100yds (91m)

from the falls, but with fine views of them, particularly from two viewpoint spurs on the right. Where the path is carved into the hillside, it shows the underlying rock, which is lumpy white quartzite. This is the same rock that gives a whitish appearance to the tops of the hills above Glen Nevis.

Above the second viewpoint, the path bends left. Here a small path runs ahead through boggy ground. This is aiming for the top of the upper fall, but it isn't recommended as the rocks alongside the fall are unsafe (wet quartzite is slippery) and you don't actually get a better view of the water.

Not far above, the path runs up to a forest road. Turn left, signed 'Car Park'. Open heather above the track is being colonised by birch and pine, and also by larch seeding itself out of the plantations below. At a junction, the downward path, which is a short-cut back to the car park, has red-and-white waymarkers. Your route turns uphill to the right, with a red waymarker.

WHERE TO EAT AND DRINK ⓘ

Nether Lochaber Hotel, at Corran Ferry, has an unpretentious bar with good food and friendly atmosphere (dogs are welcome). The furry creature above the bar is not, as one visitor described it, a 'small Scottish bear'; it's a pine marten, wearing the tie of the Newtonmore shinty team.

The wide path runs up under gloomy larches, with clearings formed by windblow. In economic terms it makes sense to keep planting, even where there is a slight risk of losing trees in this way. Unusually stormy winters in 1999 and 2000 have made trees more vulnerable than the planters of 30 years ago, before global warming, could have expected.

WHILE YOU'RE THERE ⓘ

The **West Highland Museum**, in the centre of Fort William, is old-fashioned. It's almost a museum of how museums used to be in that there are interesting items in display cases rather than screens and storyboards. There is a lock of Bonnie Prince Charlie's hair that was presumably still on his head as he marched across the Corrieyairack, as well as a secret picture of him that has to be viewed via a polished metal cylinder.

A stream runs up beside the track, which bends left to cross it. As it reaches more open ground above, it is running along the line of one of General Wade's military roads (► Walk 22). This one ran from Corran Ferry to Corrychurrachan and Fort William. There's really only one way to build a basic road without tarmac. The new path illustrates the Wade technique of jammed stones, covered with finer gravel, and shows it particularly clearly as here the jammed stones are whitish quartzite while the overlying gravel is reddish granite.

The path joins the end of a forest road, with a quarry on the left. Bear left on a crossing track and, in 100yds (91m), keep ahead as another forest track runs in from the right. Red waymarkers indicate the correct track. The wide, smooth road heads downhill, with views

along Loch Linnhe. A ravine on the left has been left to regenerate with a mixture of wild species and plantation escapees. The Sitka spruce is not native to Scotland, but the effect is pleasingly wild.

The slope above the forest road was clear-felled in 2002. A skyline cable was used to bring felled trees down the steep slope. This strong wire cable mounted on a standing tree trunk has to be high enough to keep the felled tree's butt above the ground on the way down, but not so high that the leverage pulls the standing tree down. The felled tree is hauled downhill by an operator in a tractor on the forest road. If the haul-in cable should break, the suddenly released end is very dangerous, and so the tractor cab is armoured for protection. If the haul-back cable breaks, the felled tree starts coming very fast, and the operator has to drop the sky line very quickly.

On a very steep slope like this one, the actual felling is the most skilled and demanding part of the job. Chainsaw operations are kept to a minimum – the trees are simply dropped to await the winch operation. Drop them wrong and they tangle up together, making the winch operation impossible. After clear-felling, replanting will be less purely commercial than last time around. The grey-green blocks of spruce will be broken up with larch.

The forest road bends to the right, with a bench that gives a distant view of Inchree waterfalls. Turn down left on a steep path, which soon levels out to a footbridge. On reaching buildings, keep straight ahead under a narrow tree-belt to the car park.

Walk 16

Ariundle Oakwoods and the Elements of Chemistry

Through the shades of green Sunart to the hillside site of an old lead mine.

•DISTANCE•	7 miles (11.3km)
•MINIMUM TIME•	3hrs 45min
•ASCENT / GRADIENT•	950ft (290m) ▲▲▲
•LEVEL OF DIFFICULTY•	🚶 🚶 🚶
•PATHS•	Good through woodland, sketchy on open hill, no stiles
•LANDSCAPE•	Ancient oakwood, open and remote hill ground
•SUGGESTED MAP•	aqua3 OS Explorer 391 Ardgour & Strontian
•START / FINISH•	Grid reference: NM 826633
•DOG FRIENDLINESS•	On leads in reserve (Scottish Natural Heritage may relax this; look for signs)
•PARKING•	Nature Reserve car park at Ariundle
•PUBLIC TOILETS•	Tourist information centre, Strontian

BACKGROUND TO THE WALK

What does Strontian have in common with the hamlet of Ytterby in Sweden, with Paris (Lutetia) and Copenhagen (Hafnia), with the planet Uranus and the Sun (Helios)? Chemical elements – the fundamental materials of nature. Seventeen are named after places, including ytterbium, lutetium, hafnium, uranium, helium – and strontium.

Davy the Namer

A new mineral was discovered in the lead ores of Strontian in 1793, and named strontites. Sir Humphrey Davy visited the mines in 1808 and isolated the new element strontium. Davy is remembered as the inventor of the safety lamp for miners, but he also identified and named the elements calcium, magnesium and chlorine.

Strontium (Sr) comes in at number 38 in the list of chemical elements. When heated its salts burn with a crimson flame, and it is used in making fireworks. The radioactive form strontium 90 does not occur in nature at Strontian or anywhere else, but is produced in nuclear explosions, including the Chernobyl reactor disaster. Because of its chemical similarity to calcium, strontium 90 is absorbed into the bones, where its radioactive breakdown damages the bone marrow.

The Older New York

The lead mines around Strontian, including the Bellsgrove mine reached on this walk, opened in the early 18th century. The villages around them came to be known as New York, after the York Building Company that built them. Some 60 tons of Strontian lead – one tenth of the year's output – went in 1753 to roof the new castle at Inveraray (▶ Walk 3). As the more accessible veins were worked out, these remote mines became uneconomic and eventually closed in 1871. They have been reopened in a small way for the extraction of the mineral barytes. The element barium, a chemical relative of calcium and strontium, is used in drilling muds for the oil industry.

Walk 16

The Wild Woods of the West

On its way to the lead mine and the waterfalls of Strontian Glen, the walk passes through the Ariundle National Nature Reserve. In the mountains, the native wild wood of Scotland was the Scots pine (▶ Walk 6). Here on the warm, damp sea coast, the wild wood is of oak. The Ariundle oakwood owes its survival to human interference. The livestock and deer that destroyed Scotland's forest were kept out so that the oaks could be coppiced – harvested on a seven-year cycle. The timber went to the iron smelters of Bonawe on Loch Etive and the oak bark to the tanning industry.

The wild oakwood is being repaired, with the felling out of commercial spruce. Beneath the dense canopy, it is carpeted in moss that even climbs the trees, and rich in ferns and primitive plants called liverworts. While we expect the natural world to be green, it's not often quite so green as Ariundle.

Walk 16 Directions

① From the car park, continue along the track into the oakwoods. After ½ mile (800m), a footpath turns off at a waymarker on the right. It crosses the **Strontian River** and heads upstream along it. After a pleasant ¾ mile (1.2km) it recrosses the river, following a duckboard section to rejoin the oakwood track.

② Turn right, away from the car park, to reach a high gate in a deer fence. The track immediately forks. Take the downward branch on the right to emerge into open grazings at river level. The track ends at a gate and stream.

WHERE TO EAT AND DRINK ⓘ
The **Ariundle Centre**, ½ mile (800m) from the start of the walk, has craft displays and a café with excellent home-made cakes. Dogs are welcome in the covered outdoor eating area.

---

③ Ford the stream on to a rough path. This crosses three more small streams, then forks. The lower, right-hand branch continues alongside the **Strontian River**, but the path, which is quite faint, slants up to the left to a solitary holly tree. Here it turns straight uphill for 50yds (46m), then bends right to slant up as before, passing 200yds (183m) below a bare rock knoll. The remains of wooden steps are in the path and a few cairns stand beside it. It steepens slightly to pass below a small crag with three different trees growing out of it – rowan, hazel and oak. With a large stream and waterfalls ahead, the path turns uphill and reaches the brink of the small gorge. Above the waterfalls, the slope eases and there is a footbridge down on the right which you don't cross; it acts as a useful landmark. Just above, the path reaches the broken dam wall of a former reservoir.

④ A green path runs across the slope just above. You can turn right on this, heading up beside the stream for about ¼ mile (400m). Here you will find a spoil heap; a heather bank marks the entrance to an adit – a mine tunnel running into the hill.

⑤ Return along the green path past Point ④, with the remains of the **Bellsgrove Lead Mines** above and below. The path improves into a track, following a stream down a small and slantwise side valley. As this stream turns down to the left, the track contours forward, to cross a wooded stream valley by a high footbridge above a waterfall.

WHILE YOU'RE THERE ⓘ
Ardnamurchan is one of the most green and beautiful corners of the Highlands, with empty beaches and wildlife cruises, either escorted or in hire boats. The remote Ardnamurchan Lighthouse, built in the 1840s, was designed by Alan Stevenson, the uncle of Robert Louis Stevenson. It is the westernmost point on the Scottish mainland and houses the **Kingdom of Light** visitor centre (April–October). You can see its 0.5 megawatt lens, as well as spot whales and dolphins if you're lucky.

---

⑥ A wide, smooth track continues ahead through a gate. After ½ mile (800m) it rejoins the outward route at the edge of the **nature reserve**. Follow the track back to the car park.

WHAT TO LOOK FOR ⓘ
You're unlikely to spot the shy **pine marten**, though there's a stuffed one behind the bar at the Nether Lochaber Hotel, on the mainland side of the Corran Ferry (► Walk 15). The animal is like a large furry ferret and lives in the trees, eating baby squirrels. (Given the chance, pine martens actually prefer chocolate and jam.) A notice board on the nature trail points out, after you've passed it, that the duckboard section of the path is a place where they sometimes leave droppings – imagine a very small dog that's been on a diet of black treacle and you get the idea.

The Nevis Gorge and its Waterfalls

A walk beside Scotland's Himalayan lookalike leading to an enormous waterfall.

•DISTANCE•	2½ miles (4km)
•MINIMUM TIME•	1hr 30min
•ASCENT / GRADIENT•	270ft (82m) ▲▲ ▲ ▲
•LEVEL OF DIFFICULTY•	👫 👫 👫
•PATHS•	Well-built path with drops alongside, no stiles
•LANDSCAPE•	Deep wooded gorge, wet meadow above
•SUGGESTED MAP•	aqua3 OS Explorer 392 Ben Nevis & Fort William
•START / FINISH•	Grid reference: NN 168691
•DOG FRIENDLINESS•	Off lead, beware of steep slopes alongside path
•PARKING•	Walkers' car park at end of Glen Nevis road
•PUBLIC TOILETS•	Glen Nevis Visitor Centre

BACKGROUND TO THE WALK

The Nevis Gorge, it's been said, is where Scotland pays its little tribute to the Himalayas. High walls of crag and boulder rise on either side. The path runs through a narrow gap where forest clings to the steep hillside and the river crashes below among its boulders.

Rocks Galore

Four different types of rock make up this scenery, and three of them are obvious from the walk. The crushed and ancient rocks of the Central Highlands (the Dalradian series) are mostly grey schist, but here there is also the pale-grey quartzite of Sgurr a' Mhaim, above the bend of the glen. The grinding of the continents at the time the Caledonian mountains were formed caused great bubbles of melted rock within the schist. These now appear at the surface as the granite on the lower slopes of Ben Nevis. It's grey on the outside, but pink when freshly broken or washed by streams. The granite was formed deep underground, but above it volcanoes were pouring out the black lava that now forms the summit of Ben Nevis and its formidable northern crags.

The First Fall

As the glen bends east towards the gorge, stop at the Polldubh car park (grid ref NN 145683). The first waterfall is hidden underneath the road bridge. The riverbed is the pinkish Nevis granite, cut by two dykes – vertical intrusions of volcanic rock – which the river has eroded into twin channels.

Continue up the road to its end at the second car park, where the walk starts. Glen Nevis has the rounded outline of a glacial valley. Glacier-smoothed rock below the car park has become an informal 'symbolic cemetery', commemorating those killed by the mountains they loved. Once above the gorge, the depth of the former glacier is shown by the rocks of Meall Cumhann, on the Ben Nevis (north) side. These are obviously smoothed by the ice that has passed right over the top of them.

Walk 17

Steall Fall

Steall Fall is about 300ft (91m) high. In a good winter it freezes completely and climbers ascend it in spiked crampons with an ice axe in each hand. The valley above the fall, the Allt Coire a' Mhail, once flowed gently out into a higher version of Glen Nevis. From above, it still appears to unwary walkers to do so. Ice deepened Glen Nevis by 750ft (228m). In the following 10,000 years, the side-stream has barely started its task of eroding the hanging valley down to the level of its new endpoint.

Walk 17 Directions

① It should be noted that the waterslide above the car park is the **Allt Coire Eoghainn** – if you mistake it for the Steall Fall and set off towards it you are on a difficult and potentially dangerous path. The path you will take on this walk is much easier, but even here there

have been casualties, mostly caused by people wearing unsuitable shoes. At the top end of the car park you will see a signpost that shows no destination closer than the 13 miles (21km) to Kinlochleven – accordingly, this walk will be a short out-and-back. The well-made path runs gently uphill under woods of birch and hazel, across what turns into a very steep slope.

For a few steps it becomes a rock-cut ledge, with a step across a waterfall side-stream. The path at this point is on clean pink granite, but you will see a boulder of grey schist beside the path just afterwards. Ahead, the top of the **Steall Fall** can now be seen through the notch of the valley.

② The path continues briefly downhill to cross a second stream; the rock now is schist, with fine zig-zag stripes of grey and white. A short rock staircase leads to a wooden balcony section. From here the path is just above the bed of the **Nevis Gorge**. The river runs through huge boulders, some of which bridge it completely.

③ Quite suddenly, the path emerges on to a level meadow above the gorge. Ahead, the Steall Fall fills the view. The best path runs along the left-hand edge of the meadow to a point opposite the waterfall.

④ The walk ends here, beside a footbridge which consists simply of

three steel cables over a very deep pool. Those who wish to attempt the crossing should note that it gets wobblier in the middle; it's hard to turn round, but the return journey is rather easier. From the wire bridge, the driest path runs alongside the main river round one bend before heading up to the foot of the waterfall. The view from directly beneath is even more spectacular.

Half Ben Nevis

The half-way lochan and the great north corrie of Nevis.

•DISTANCE•	10 miles (16.1km)
•MINIMUM TIME•	6hrs 15min
•ASCENT / GRADIENT•	2,000ft (610m) ▲▲▲
•LEVEL OF DIFFICULTY•	👫 👫 👫
•PATHS•	Hill paths, well-built, then very rough, 6 stiles
•LANDSCAPE•	Slopes of Britain's biggest hill
•SUGGESTED MAP•	aqua3 OS Explorer 392 Ben Nevis & Fort William
•START / FINISH•	Grid reference: NN 123731
•DOG FRIENDLINESS•	On leads through Achintee grazings, by River Nevis
•PARKING•	Large car park at Glen Nevis Visitor Centre
•PUBLIC TOILETS•	At start

BACKGROUND TO THE WALK

For 21 years in the 19th century, an observatory was sited on the summit of Ben Nevis. It recorded, to the surprise of few, that this is one of the wettest spots in Britain. Averaged over the year, the summit is sunny for about two hours per day.

This walk of half the hill shows you the mountain's great northern crags and the rocky hollow of Coire Leis. The further edge of the corrie is the jagged line of Tower Ridge, Britain's longest rock climb. In early spring the damp Atlantic winds coat the crags in thick hoar-frost, over which climbers with crampons and ice axes have created hundreds of routes.

Chamber of Clouds

Charles Wilson, a grammar school teacher turned Cambridge professor, came to Ben Nevis on holiday in 1894. The Scottish-born professor was so struck by the effects of sunlight on the clouds above Coire Leis that he attempted to reproduce them in the Cavendish Laboratory. In so doing he invented the Wilson cloud chamber, for which he was awarded the Nobel Prize for Physics in 1927.

In summer, the moist Atlantic air that sweeps into Coire Leis condenses into cloud, and then rain. Each droplet forms around a 'nucleation centre' such as a speck of dust. Perfectly clean air can become supersaturated: it has more than enough moisture to form clouds, but can't. When moist air rises up Ben Nevis it expands due to the drop in pressure. As it expands it cools, allowing the water droplets to appear. In Wilson's Cloud Chamber, the pressure drop was achieved by means of a bicycle pump working backwards. One pull of the pump handle, and any passing particle became suddenly visible as a pencil-line of white cloud. The step-up in size is astonishing: it's as if a small model aeroplane left a vapour trail as wide as the solar system and visible to an observer on another star!

Cosmic rays – high energy particles from outer space – can be seen zipping through the cloud chamber. Thus the positron (the positive electron) was discovered in 1932 and the muon (an exotic heavy electron) in 1937. It is actually possible to make your own Wilson cloud chamber – simply cool air with dry ice and shine a torch in. The successor to the cloud chamber was devised while gazing into a glass of beer. Donald Glaser earned the Nobel Prize for his bubble chamber in 1960.

Walk 18 Directions

① At the downstream corner of the car park, a bridge signed 'Ben Path' crosses the **River Nevis**. The path turns upstream, crossing fields to join the **Mountain Trail** (formerly known as the Pony Track) to Ben Nevis. After a long climb, a notice points you to a zig-zag up left on to the half-way plateau. The path passes above **Lochan Meall an-t-Suidhe**, the Halfway Lochan, down on the left.

② The main path takes a sharp turn back to the right, heading for the summit. Your smaller path descends ahead, behind a wall-like cairn. Soon it climbs gently over peat bog to a cairn on the skyline. Here it becomes rough and rocky as it slants down across the steep slide slope of the valley of **Allt a' Mhuilinn**. Eventually it joins the stream and runs up beside it to the **Charles Inglis Clark (CIC) Hut**.

③ Return for 100yds (91m) and cross the stream on the right to join a clear path which leads downhill. This descends a rocky step with a waterslide and reaches a ladder stile into plantations.

④ Go down a forest road and where it bends left over a bridge, keep ahead down a rough path. This stays beside the stream to a ladder stile at the railbed of the old aluminium railway. Turn left for ½ mile (800m), when a side-track joins from the left and the track passes under power lines. In another 220yds (201m) take a smaller track on the right that rejoins the **Allt a' Mhuilinn**. Keep to the right of distillery buildings to reach the **A82**.

⑤ Cross the **River Lochy** on **Victoria Bridge** opposite and turn left into a fenced-off side road and left again along a street. It rises to a railway bridge. Turn left here on to a long footbridge back across the Lochy. At its end, turn right over a stile for a riverside path. This passes to the right of a rugby ground, then becomes a built path into woodland. After two footbridges, bear left on a smaller path to the edge of **Inverlochy**. Turn right, then left into a street with copper beeches. This leads through **Montrose Square** to the **A82**.

⑥ The street opposite is signed 'Ben Nevis Footpath'. Shortly, take a stone bridge to the **Glen Nevis road**. Turn left for ¼ mile (400m) to a track on the left. Recross the **Nevis** on a green footbridge and turn right to a lay-by marked 'No Overnight Parking'. Just beyond this a small riverside footpath leads up-river to the footbridge at **Glen Nevis Visitor Centre**.

The Peat Road to Cow Hill

Another loop looking down at Fort William and up at Ben Nevis.
See map and information panel for Walk 18

•DISTANCE•	7¼ miles (11.7km)
•MINIMUM TIME•	3hrs 30min
•ASCENT / GRADIENT•	1,000ft (305m) ▲▲▲
•LEVEL OF DIFFICULTY•	🚶 🚶 🚶

Walk 19 Directions
(Walk 18 option)

From the **Glen Nevis Visitor Centre** (Point ① of Walk 18), follow the riverbank to a footbridge signed 'Ben Path'. Cross and follow a small path to the left, downstream. With the road just ahead, a riverside path forks off to the left. This has one boggy section and an awkward stride across a side stream, so the road alongside is an alternative. The path and road rejoin after ½ mile (800m) and lead down to a green metal footbridge (Point Ⓐ).

Cross and turn right, down the **Glen Nevis road** to a roundabout and go left into **Fort William**. Bear right past the entrance to the station. Here an underpass on the left leads into the main street, but the walk bears right, across the front of the Safeway supermarket to a roundabout. Beyond is the old fort (Point Ⓑ), now serving as the start point for the new **Great Glen Way**. The lochside pavement leads to a car park.

From the far corner of the car park (Point Ⓒ), cross the **A82** and go up to the right of a school to join a tarred path under trees. This leads

up to **Lundavra Road**. Turn uphill to the top of the town and across a cattle grid with a kissing gate alongside to a gate on the left signed 'Keep Clear 24hr Access' (Point Ⓓ). This is the **Peat Road**, originally formed by sledges bringing peat for fuel down off the hill. It rises over the moor to bend left past a tall waymarker (Point Ⓔ). Continue along the smooth track to the summit of **Cow Hill**, which has views down on to Fort William and along Loch Linnhe and Loch Eil.

Return down the track to the waymarker (Point Ⓔ). Turn left (**Peat Road**) and follow a well-made path down into woodland. It descends steeply to reach a forest road. Go straight across to a continuing path with the thistle waymarker of the **West Highland Way**. At the valley floor, an old burial ground is up on the left (Point Ⓕ) with a gate and footbridge giving access to it. It is worth visiting for its atmospheric beeches and table tombs of the early 19th century. The main path soon leads to the **Glen Nevis road**.

Turn left along the pavement for 100yds (91m) and cross to a footpath under trees to return to the visitor centre.

Banks of the Caledonian

A walk along – and underneath – Telford's masterpiece of civil engineering.

•DISTANCE•	4½ miles (7.2km)
•MINIMUM TIME•	1hr 45min
•ASCENT / GRADIENT•	100ft (30m)
•LEVEL OF DIFFICULTY•	
•PATHS•	Wide tow paths, no stiles
•LANDSCAPE•	Banks of wide canal and shore of tidal Loch Lochy
•SUGGESTED MAP•	aqua3 OS Explorer 392 Ben Nevis & Fort William
•START / FINISH•	Grid reference: NN 096768
•DOG FRIENDLINESS•	Sensible dogs off-lead on tow path
•PARKING•	At Kilmallie Hall, Corpach
•PUBLIC TOILETS•	At start

Walk 20 Directions

Scotland's great coast-to-coast canal, opened in 1822, is just one of the masterpieces of civil engineering by Thomas Telford. The poet laureate Robert Southey (1774–1843) referred to Telford as 'Pontifex Maximus', the Biggest Bridge-builder. As well as the old-style stone bridge, Telford became a master of two entirely new techniques – the cast-iron arch and the first suspension bridges. While working on the canal, he was also building 600 miles (around 965km) of new roads and enlarging most of Scotland's harbours.

WHAT TO LOOK FOR

From Fort William, Britain's biggest hill appears as a mere hump. The canalside, however, gives the best view into the northern corrie of **Ben Nevis**. On its right-hand side rise the buttresses of the country's largest crag, one behind the other. Across the back is a narrow edge of granite, linking it to the neighbouring Carn Mor Dearg. This arête is the mountaineers route on to the big Ben.

Go down past **Corpach Station** to Telford's great canal and cross the lowest lock that separates salt water (right) from fresh (left). Turn left to reach two more locks.

Work on the canal started in 1803, during the Napoleonic War, and each of its 29 locks is designed to take a 40-gun frigate of Nelson's navy. Roughly 200 million wheelbarrow loads of earth were shifted over the next 19 years.

Just after the second lock, a path on the right has a blue footpath sign and a Great Glen Way marker. It passes under tall sycamores to the shore. Follow the shoreline path past a football pitch, then turn left across damp grass to a road sign that warns motorists of a nearby playground. A path ahead leads up a wooded bank to the tow path.

Turn right along the tow path for ½ mile (800m). Just before the **Banavie swing bridge**, a path down to the right has a Great Glen Way waymarker. Follow these waymarkers on street signs to a

> **WHERE TO EAT AND DRINK** ⓘ
> The **Moorings Inn** at Banavie offers bar meals and a restaurant. On the other side of the A830 and canal, the **Lochy** family pub has picnic tables and serves 'massive portions'. Dogs are welcome in the bar, but not the restaurant.

level crossing and turn left towards the other swing bridge, the one with the road on it.

In 1996, the government promised £20 million for a complete refurbishment: 'Canals have a great future.' For those without boats, the tow path has been resurfaced as a cycleway from coast to coast, with a new National Trail, the Great Glen Way, running parallel. Before the swing bridge, turn right at signs for the Great Glen Way and cycle route.

The 60ft (18m) height gain along the eight locks of Neptune's Staircase is the serious uphill part of this walk, but more serious for boats. It takes 90 minutes to work through the system. The canal is fairly busy, with pleasure yachts, fishing boats crossing from the Minch to their east coast home ports and the *Lord of the Glen* steamer. You should get the chance to see the locks in operation. As each one fills, slow roiling currents come up from underneath, like bathwater emptying but in reverse. As it empties, water emerges from the masonry in little fountains.

A gate marks the top of the locks. About 200yds (183m) later a gate on the right leads to a dump for dead cars; ignore this one. The canal crosses a wooded valley, with a black fence on the right, to reach a second gate. Go through, to a track turning back sharply right and descending to ford a small stream.

Up on the right, the stream passes right under the canal in an arched tunnel. Beside it is a second tunnel, which provides you with a way to the other side. A small amount of water from the canal drips into the tunnel, which has a fairly spooky atmosphere. Four aqueducts let streams and rivers pass below the waterway. Other works included a dam on Loch Lochy and diversion of the rivers Oich and Lochy. Loch Oich needed to be deepened, and for this task a steam dredger had not only to be built, but invented and designed. And before a single turf was shifted, the first essential was a brewery to supply the thousands of navvies. At the tunnel's end, a track runs up to join the canal's northern tow path.

> **WHILE YOU'RE THERE** ⓘ
> Much to Thomas Telford's distress, the canal was a loss-making enterprise from the day it opened. One reason was the coming of the railways. At Banavie, the West Highland Railway is Britain's most beautiful. During the summer, the steam-powered **Jacobite Steam Train** runs daily (except Saturdays) to Mallaig and back; there's a stop-off on the way to admire the viaduct and rail museum at Glenfinnan.

Turn right, with the canal now on your left, back past the quays of **Neptune's Staircase**. At their foot, cross the **A830** to a level crossing (path crossing only, no warning lights). Continue along the right-hand tow path. On the right, wet meadows below the level of the canal sparkle in spring with yellow flag iris, followed in early summer by typical wet meadow flowers such as pink valerian and white meadowsweet. After a mile (1.6km) the tow path track leads back to the **Corpach** double lock.

A Happy Birch-day in Coire Ardair

Regenerating woodlands lead to a high pass where Bonnie Prince Charlie escaped through the window.

•DISTANCE•	8 miles (12.9km)
•MINIMUM TIME•	4hrs 15min
•ASCENT / GRADIENT•	1,400ft (427m) ▲▲▲
•LEVEL OF DIFFICULTY•	🚶🚶 🚶🚶 🚶
•PATHS•	Mostly good, wet and stony in places, no stiles
•LANDSCAPE•	One-ended valley leading to lochan under crags
•SUGGESTED MAP•	aqua3 OS Explorer 401 Loch Laggan & Creag Meagaidh
•START / FINISH•	Grid reference: NN 483872
•DOG FRIENDLINESS•	No dogs allowed as they disturb wildlife
•PARKING•	Nature reserve car park at Aberarder track end beside Loch Laggan
•PUBLIC TOILETS•	None on route or near by

BACKGROUND TO THE WALK

As the path curves westward after Point ②, you'll see the crags of Creag Meagaidh. When well iced up, these create many famous winter climbs. On the right, they're bounded by a narrow pass high on the skyline.

Bonnie Prince Charlie

After the defeat of the Jacobite cause at Culloden Moor on 16 April, 1746, Prince Charles Edward Stuart went on the run in the Scottish Highlands. From then until 18 September, he sheltered in caves and bothies (shepherds' huts) and in the open heather. He was often hungry, usually wet, hunted by redcoat soldiers and plagued by midges.

His flight took him across the country to Mallaig, for an 80-mile (129km) journey by open boat in a storm to the Outer Hebrides. He came back to Skye disguised as the maidservant of Miss Flora MacDonald. The prince adapted well to the life of a long-distance backpacker, living for weeks in the same dirty shirt and greasy black kilt, growing a long red beard and learning to enjoy the oat bread and whisky of the country. In a bothy on South Uist, he out-drank all of his companions and then intoned a penitential psalm over their unconscious bodies.

In the face of the weather and a barbarous and implacable enemy, he showed not just strength and courage, but good humour as well. He made jokes with Flora MacDonald – 'they'll never guess what I've got hidden up my skirts' (it was a pistol).

The prince came to know Scotland like no monarch before or since, and at the same time, Scotland's people – from clan chieftains to crofters and fishermen, and even outlaws like the Seven Men of Glenmoriston. Despite a price on his head of £30,000, equivalent to more than a lottery jackpot of today, not one of them betrayed him.

Back on the mainland, in July he was encircled by Hanoverian soldiers, but slipped between two sentries in the dark. By mid-August the manhunt had been abandoned. Soon afterwards he heard of a French boat waiting near Mallaig. Travelling away from the main roads, on 18 September he passed along the route of the walk, up to Coire Ardair and then through the high pass alongside Creag Meagaidh into the empty country around Glen Roy. That pass is called Uinneag Coire Ardair. Translating it into English we can say that Prince Charlie left Scotland through the Window.

Walk 21 Directions

① A grey gravel track leads to **Aberarder farm**. Here an information area includes a picnic table conveniently placed under a rainproof roof. Pass to the right of the buildings following a footprint waymarker on to a rebuilt path.

② The path rises through bracken, then crosses a boggy area on old railway sleepers. It heads up the

Walk 21

valley of **Allt Coire Ardair**, keeping a little way up the right-hand side, becoming fairly rocky and rugged as it ascends through an area of regenerating birch trees. Now the crags of **Coire Ardair** come into sight ahead. The path crosses many small streams then bends left, slightly downhill, to join the main river. Tiny rowan trees can be seen attempting to regenerate among the heather. Wild flowers in the boggy ground include the pink or white pyramids of the heath spotted orchid (the leaves have the spots). A peaty area, crossed on railway sleepers, leads up suddenly to the outflow of **Lochan a' Choire**.

WHILE YOU'RE THERE

The **Highland Folk Museum** at Newtonmore is the site of Baile Gean, a working reconstruction of an 18th-century township where you can immerse yourself in the peat reek of a rebuilt traditional black house with heather-thatched roof and smoke-stained walls. There's also a 1930s working croft, a joiner's workshop and a school. The site is so large that some pre-war buses have been refitted to take you round it.

WHERE TO EAT AND DRINK

Scotland has few pubs, and the traditional drinking place has always been the bar of the local hotel. Laggan's **Monadhliath Hotel** caters mainly for locals, but serves good bar meals to visitors too (children and dogs welcome). It's a former manse, easily recognised by the ruined church in its garden.

③ The outflow is a fine viewpoint for the crag walls of **Coire Ardair**. These walls are too loose and overgrown for rock climbing, but when covered in snow and hoarfrost give excellent sport for winter mountaineers. The circuit of the lochan is considerably more rugged than the path up the glen, and could be omitted if the outflow stream is too full, or if a picnic is preferred. Cross the outflow stream near where it emerges from the

lochan and follow a small path round the shore to the notable clump of boulders marked by a stretcher box. (The stretcher is used for removing mountain casualties from the foot of the crags.) One of the boulders forms a small cave, with a spring running through it. A vigorous rowan tree, seeded where deer can't get at it, shows that without grazing pressure this glen would be wooded even at this altitude of 2,000ft (610m).

④ After the boulder cave you must cross rocks and scree. This short section is awkward. Once past the head of the lochan, slant up away from the shore. A path descends from high on the left, coming out of the notch called the **Window**. Join this and turn down to the loch's outflow (Point ③ again). Quite clearly there's no way out of this dead-end valley that doesn't involve serious mountain walking – or one of those winter climbs up the icy gullies. Return down the valley by the outward path.

WHAT TO LOOK FOR

The natural forest of the lower slopes of Scotland is the **birch**. In Creag Meagaidh Reserve, deer numbers are being carefully controlled by shooting to allow the woodland to regenerate without the use of fencing. Early on the path, a signboard shows the treeless slopes as they were in 1986 – they're greener now. Further up, the path passes through young birches. If it's been raining, these will give you a good soaking from the waist down. Further up the corrie, just a few tiny rowans are struggling out of the heather.

Up and Down the Corrieyairack

Above the Great Glen on the road the English built and Bonnie Prince Charlie marched over.

•DISTANCE•	7¼ miles (11.7km)
•MINIMUM TIME•	4hrs
•ASCENT / GRADIENT•	1,300ft (395m) ▲▲▲
•LEVEL OF DIFFICULTY•	林林 林林 林林
•PATHS•	Tracks, one vanished pathless section, 2 stiles
•LANDSCAPE•	Foothills of Monadhliath, birchwood hollows
•SUGGESTED MAP•	aqua3 OS Explorer 400 Loch Lochy & Glen Roy
•START / FINISH•	Grid reference: NH 378080
•DOG FRIENDLINESS•	Off lead, unless passing sheep
•PARKING•	Southern edge of Fort Augustus, signed lane leads off A82 to burial ground
•PUBLIC TOILETS•	Fort Augustus

BACKGROUND TO THE WALK

The most striking feature of Scotland's geography is the 2,000ft (610m) deep Great Glen. It runs perfectly straight from Fort William to Inverness as if a giant ploughshare had been dragged across the country.

Scotland's San Andreas

Around 400 million years ago, the northern part of Scotland slipped 65 miles (105km) to the left. Looking across from Corrieyairack, you'd have seen ground that's now the Island of Mull. The Great Glen represents a tear-fault, similar to the San Andreas Fault in California, but no longer active, so that there isn't going to be any Fort Augustus Earthquake. Where two ground masses slide past each other, the rock where they touch is shattered. Rivers and glaciers have worn away this broken rock to make the striking valley.

Wade's Ways

After the uprising of 1715, General Wade became the military commander of Scotland. He constructed and repaired forts along the Great Glen at Fort William, Fort Augustus and Inverness, as well as at Ruthven on the present A9 and Glenelg (► Walk 31). To link them, he built 260 miles (around 418km) of roads across the Highlands. The most spectacular of these was the one through the Corrieyairack Pass, rising to 2,500ft (762m) to link the Great Glen with the Spey.

The construction was little changed since Roman times. Large rocks were jammed together into a firm bed, up to 15ft (4.5m) wide, and then surfaced with smaller stones and gravel packed down. Modern path-builders know that however well you build it, if it's got water running down it turns into a stream. Wade paid particular attention to drainage. The 500 soldiers working through the summer of 1731 got a bonus of 6d a day – about £5 in today's money – and celebrated its completion with a barbecue of six oxen.

The chieftains worried that the roads would soften their people, making them unfit for raids across rough country. But they soon came to appreciate the convenience. 'If you'd seen these roads before they were made, You'd lift up your hands and bless General Wade.'

And when Prince Charles Stuart landed 14 years later, it was the Jacobite army that marched triumphantly across the Corrieyairack. At the Speyside end of the pass, a small and ill-prepared force under General John Cope fled before him into England. And a new Wade rhyme was inserted, temporarily, into the National Anthem itself: 'God grant that Marshal Wade, May by Thy mighty aid, Victory bring, May he sedition hush, and like a torrent rush, Rebellious Scots to crush, God save the King.'

Walk 22 **Directions**

① A track leads round to left of the burial ground to meet a minor road. Turn right for about ¼ mile (400m) to the foot of a rather rubbly track signposted for the Corrieyairack Pass. After some 50yds (46m) the track passes through a gate, getting much easier, and, soon, the right of way joins a smoother track coming up from **Culachy House**.

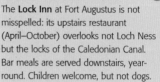

② After another ¼ mile (400m), a gate leads out on to the open hill. About 350yds (320m) further on, the track passes under high-tension wires. At once bear left across a grassy meadow. As this drops towards a stream, you will see a green track slanting down to the right. Bear left off the track to pass the corner of a deer fence, where a small path continues down to the stream. Cross and turn downstream on an old grassy track. It recrosses the stream and passes under the high power line to a bend with a sudden view across deep and wooded **Glen Tarff**.

> ### WHILE YOU'RE THERE ⓘ
> You will find a rather specialised take on the life of the Highlanders at the **Clansman Centre** in Fort Augustus, which focuses on their techniques of doing away with one another. In a simulated turf house, staff will teach the 'art of killing or maiming using ancient weapons', and will even make the weapons for you themselves.

③ Turn right across a high stone bridge. A disused track climbs through birch woods then, as a terraced shelf, across the high side of Glen Tarff. A side stream forms a wooded re-entrant ahead. The old track contours in to this and crosses below a narrow waterfall – the former bridge has disappeared.

④ Contour out across the steep slope to pick up the old track as it restarts. It runs gently uphill to a gateless gateway in a fence. Turn up the fence to another gateway, 150yds (137m) above. Here turn left for 20yds (18m) to the brink of another stream hollow. (Its delightful Gaelic name – Sidhean Ceum na Goibhre – means 'Fairy Goat-step'.) Don't go into this, but

> ### WHERE TO EAT AND DRINK ⓘ
> The **Lock Inn** at Fort Augustus is not misspelled: its upstairs restaurant (April–October) overlooks not Loch Ness but the locks of the Caledonian Canal. Bar meals are served downstairs, year-round. Children welcome, but not dogs.

turn uphill alongside it, through pathless bracken, to its top. A deer fence is just above; turn left alongside it to go through a nearby gate, then left beside the fence. When it turns downhill, a green path continues ahead, gently uphill through heather. Far ahead and above, pylons crossing the skyline mark the **Corrieyairack Pass**. The path bends right to join the Corrieyairack track just above.

⑤ Turn right. The track passes a knoll on the right where a small cairn marks the highest point of this walk. It then descends in sweeping curves for 1¼ miles (2km). The pass is still technically a road, and where it crosses a stream, a Highways Authority sign warns motorists coming up it of the various difficulties and dangers ahead. From here the track climbs gently to rejoin the upward route. At the final bend, a stile offers a short cut through (rather than round) the ancient burial ground.

> ### WHAT TO LOOK FOR ⓘ
> Despite the road's preservation as an ancient monument, you will see little of General Wade's work, apart from its ambitious uphill line preserved by the modern track on top. You may be more interested by the **burial ground** at the start of the walk. Here is buried 'John Anderson, my Jo', subject of a sentimental poem by Robert Burns; and Gilleasbuig MacDonald, bard of North Uist, who died on his way to visit his publisher in Inverness.

Moorland on Morrone

The hill at the back of Braemar gives a taste of the Cairngorms.

•DISTANCE•	6¾ miles (10.9km)
•MINIMUM TIME•	4hrs 15min
•ASCENT / GRADIENT•	2,000ft (610m) ▲ ▲ ▲
•LEVEL OF DIFFICULTY•	🚶 🚶 🚶
•PATHS•	Well-made but fairly steep path, track, 1 stile
•LANDSCAPE•	Rolling heather hills
•SUGGESTED MAP•	aqua3 OS Explorer 387 Glen Shee & Braemar
•START / FINISH•	Grid reference: NO 143911
•DOG FRIENDLINESS•	On leads in reserve, also on hill during grouse nesting May/June
•PARKING•	Duck Pond, at top of Chapel Brae, Braemar
•PUBLIC TOILETS•	Braemar centre (opposite Fife Arms)

BACKGROUND TO THE WALK

Coming down the back of Morrone Hill, you descend through several different plant zones, and the home ground of two distinctive Grampian birds.

Ptarmigan Pterritory

On the windswept, often snow-covered summit plateau, gravel alternates with shrubby plants that grow barely ankle-high. These are food for the ptarmigan, a bird of the grouse family that's rather like a small hen. Uniquely among British birds it turns white in the winter, and in spring and early summer it will still be white in patches. Its late summer plumage is paler than the grouse, and more speckled. But the easy way to recognise it is by where it lives – a grouse above the heather line is a ptarmigan – and by its behaviour. It relies on camouflage, and when you notice it, will probably be standing on the gravel only a few yards away. Even then, it doesn't fly away, but will probably wander off round the back of a boulder. In springtime, the male bird's soaring display flight is accompanied by a soundtrack of belches and cackles. The 'P' at the beginning of its name is purely ornamental – in Gaelic it's tarmachan.

Heather and Grouse

At the 2,000ft (610m) mark, bilberry and some grass grow, along with dwarf heather. Once you turn down on to slightly more sheltered ground, the heather springs up twice as high. At around 1,500ft (457m), it is deep enough to hinder off-path walking. Wild flowers like yellow tormentil and white woodruff are established, and you may see meadow pipits and mountain hare.

A small brown bird – or more likely three or four – leaps up out of the heather with a squawking cry that seems to say 'go back, go back!' Grouse go with heather, like pandas go with bamboo and koalas with gum trees. Red grouse are found only in the British Isles, and unfortunately their heather country, however familiar and tiresome to Scottish walkers, is rare and vanishing in a world context. The grouse need old leggy heather to nest in, but shorter, younger plants to eat. As a result, grouse moors are burnt in a ten-year cycle to provide tall heather with short fresh heather near by. The piebald effect of 'muirburn', as it's called, gives these lumpy hills an attractive extra texture.

Eighty per cent of the grouse's diet is heather, the rest being the insects that live in it. As birds lack teeth they require small stones in their gizzards to help grind their food up and aid digestion. For grouse, sharp quartz grit is ideal, and you may spot small piles of this beside the track.

Walk 23 Directions

① Take the wide track uphill, to the right of the duck pond at the top of **Chapel Brae**, bearing left twice to **Woodhill house**. The house can be bypassed by taking a small footpath on the right which rejoins the track just above. When the track forks again, bear left to a viewpoint indicator.

Walk 23

② Cross a track diagonally to a hill path marked 'Morrone'. The path has been rebuilt with rough stone steps. Higher up, it slants to the right along a line of rocky outcrops, a geological dyke of harder rock. At the top of this it turns directly uphill, passing five sprawling cairns. These are the turning point in the Morrone Hill Race that is part of the Braemar Games. The wide, stony path runs up to the **radio mast** and other ugly constructions on the summit.

WHERE TO EAT AND DRINK ⓘ

The Duke of Fife used to own all Braemar west of the River Clunie. 'He is immensely rich,' said Queen Victoria with approval when he wanted to marry her daughter. The **Fife Arms**, with the standard hewn pine trunks along its frontage, has a large bar full of hillwalkers (and their dogs, on leads). Bar meals are served in walker-size portions.

---

③ The summit, if you turn your back on the buildings, has fine views across Deeside to the high Cairngorms. On the main tops, Ben Macdui and Beinn a' Bhuird, snow may show right through the summer. To the east you will see Loch Callater and the White Mounth plateau. A notable hump is Cac Carn Beag, one of the summits of Lochnagar. Morrone's summit area is bare stones, but if you go past the buildings you'll find the start of a wide track. It runs down to a shallow col and climbs to the cairn on the low summit beyond. Here it bends left towards a lower col, but before reaching it, turns left again down the side of the hill. A gentle zig-zagging descent leads to the road by the **Clunie Water**.

④ Turn left, alongside the river, for 1½ miles (2.4km). Ben Avon with its row of summit tors fills the skyline ahead. After a snow gate and golf clubhouse comes a road sign warning of a cattle grid (the grid itself is round the next bend). Here a track, back up to the left, has a blue-topped waymarker pole.

⑤ Go up between caravans to a ladder stile with dog flap. A faint path leads up under birches, bearing right and becoming clearer. After a gate in a fence the path becomes quite clear, leading to a Scottish Natural Heritage signboard and blue waymarker at the top of the birchwood. The path becomes a track with a fence on its right and, in 220yds (201m), reaches the viewpoint indicator, Point ②. Here you can either return to the duck pond, or continue on Walk 24.

WHAT TO LOOK FOR ⓘ

The tundra shrubs that grow on the plateau belong to the heather family, but with oval leaves rather than needles. They can be distinguished easily from August as their berries are conveniently colour-coded. The **crowberry** fruit is black, the **cowberry** red and the **bilberry**, also known as whortleberry and blaeberry, has a juicy purple fruit and pale green leaves. Ptarmigan droppings are stained purple with this fruit, which is also tasty to humans.

WHILE YOU'RE THERE ⓘ

Braemar Castle is smaller, older and to my eye much more attractive than Balmoral, where the Queen lives. It was an important strong point, replacing the even older ruin alongside the River Clunie just above the bridge. Its surrounding wall is a later improvement, designed to cope with attackers during the age of the musket. Inside it has the world's largest cairngorm (a semi-precious stone), and underneath there's a pit dungeon for miscreants.

Morrone Birkwood

Circle Braemar by an ancient woodland and a royal river.
See map and information panel for Walk 23

•DISTANCE•	5½ miles (8.8km)
•MINIMUM TIME•	2hrs 15min
•ASCENT / GRADIENT•	500ft (152m) ▲▲ ▲
•LEVEL OF DIFFICULTY•	林林 林林 林林

Walk 24 Directions
(Walk 23 option)

From Point ① head back towards the village for about 400yds (366m). Turn left past a large larch down to a car park (Point Ⓐ) and cross to the **River Dee**. Turn right, downstream, between the river and a fence. Ignore a ladder stile on the right and continue to where the **Clunie Water** flows in (Point Ⓑ).

Follow the bank over a slippery stone flood barrier and head upstream beside the Clunie. The path becomes quite narrow and awkward, particularly if trodden by cows. After ¾ mile (1.2km), a footbridge leads across to a car park opposite the **Invercauld Hotel** (Point Ⓒ).

Turn right and cross the bridge towards **Braemar** village centre, but at once turn left on to a minor road. It heads upstream past the ruins of the **Old Braemar Castle**. After ¾ mile (1.2km) it crosses a cattle grid to a track on the right (Point ⑤).

Follow Walk 23 up to the viewpoint indicator (Point ②). Keep on the main track ahead; in 50yds (46m) it

bears left and contours through birchwood with juniper. After a mile (1.6km), the track reaches a gate with a ladder stile alongside (Point Ⓓ).

Don't cross into the plantation ahead, but turn sharp right on a small path with a blue waymarker. It stays close to the plantation fence for 100yds (91m), then bears right for the same distance. Now it bends right again and passes a damper area on the right, which is grass not heather. Opposite the far end of this green patch, a small path turns up to the left, across the top of a low knoll and down towards the Dee. It crosses slabs of bare rock (Point Ⓔ), a fine viewpoint and picnic place.

Continue down a slight spur, passing a small pool in the trees on the right, then bearing right. The path now runs level, with the Dee Valley down on its left. It crosses a stream, then a wider path joins from the right and you cross another stream with stepping stones. The path is wide and clear now to a kissing gate in a deer fence. Further on is a track junction (Point Ⓕ) near the duck pond.

Go straight on here to return to the car park.

Balmoral Castle and the Dee

A walk past the Queen's memorials to her husband, servants and dogs.

•DISTANCE•	4¾ miles (7.7km)
•MINIMUM TIME•	2hrs 30min
•ASCENT / GRADIENT•	800ft (244m) ▲▲▲
•LEVEL OF DIFFICULTY•	👫 👫 👫
•PATHS•	Tracks and paths, no stiles
•LANDSCAPE•	Pine forest and viewpoints above wide river valley
•SUGGESTED MAP•	aqua3 OS Explorer 388 Lochnagar
•START / FINISH•	Grid reference: NO 264949
•DOG FRIENDLINESS•	On lead in castle grounds
•PARKING•	Large pay-and-display at Crathie Church
•PUBLIC TOILETS•	Balmoral Castle
•NOTE•	Access available Easter to end July only – Royal Family in residence from August

Walk 25 Directions

From the car park, cross the **River Dee** to the lodge gateway into **Balmoral Castle**. You must pay to enter the grounds and can also buy a booklet with a map of the marked walks. Shortly, turn right off the driveway on a track that bends to the left as it reaches the river. After 200yds (183m) bear left on a path that continues along the riverbank. At a yellow waymarker turn left, past a red pillar box to the cafeteria.

Go round to the left of the castle to its east front. This has a plaque of St Hubert, patron saint of hunters. Hubert's message is actually to spare the deer, but this was lost on Prince Albert, who used to blaze away at them out of the castle windows. A path runs directly away from the castle, to the right of a sunken rose garden, past the memorials to dogs. At a path junction turn right through a pinewood to regain the riverside.

Turn left on the riverside path. The tall white flowers of angelica grow here, releasing a smell like aniseed; there are lupins too, whose seeds are carried here by the river. The path runs up to a tarred driveway, which you follow for 55yds (50m) to a path rising on the left. This crosses another driveway and rises through the woods to a junction with a map showing the estate paths.

Turn up to the right on a track that steepens and bends to the left under larches. At its highest point it reaches a T-junction.

> **WHILE YOU'RE THERE**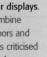
> Entering the castle grounds, you've already paid to visit the **indoor displays**. Victoria and Albert liked to combine tartan wallpaper with tartan floors and decorate with thistles. This was criticised even at the time and has now been moderated. Even so, the pictures, mostly stags in landscapes, and precious objects show a Victorian gusto and a touch of vulgarity that's refreshingly different from today's taste.

Walk 25

Turn right for the fine view ahead into the corrie of Lochnagar. This mountain dominates Balmoral and was a favourite of Queen Victoria. Her great-great-grandson, Prince Charles, also admires it and has made it the setting for his children's book *The Old Man of Lochnagar*.

The little-used track runs down to join an unsurfaced forest road where you turn left. A deer fence on the right is threaded with thin laths, designed to make it visible to capercaillie. Injury from flying into fences is a significant reason for the decline of this handsome, and now almost extinct, large grouse.

> **WHAT TO LOOK FOR** ⓘ
> You will pass some quite unexpected **statues** of animals. In the course of the walk you should spot a chamois, a wild boar and a collie dog. Also of interest are the castle's odd outbuildings, including many green wooden sentry boxes and a circular game larder which is decorated with antlers.

After a gate in the deer fence, turn right at a triangle junction, up a new forest road. In about 350yds (320m), a wide path turns up to the left and leads to a huge pyramidal **cairn**. It was raised 'to the beloved memory of Albert the great and good; prince consort. Erected by his broken-hearted widow'. Victoria and six of her children placed stones bearing their initials in its base. It has wide views in many directions, though not to the castle itself, which is concealed by trees.

The path continues on the right, descending quite steeply to a corner where trees have been felled to provide a view down the Dee. Queen Victoria raised ugly stonework even on supposedly

joyous occasions, and the next cairn, massive and conical, celebrates the marriage of her daughter, Princess Alice, to Prince Henry of Battenberg. The path descends through the deer fence to a tarred estate road. Opposite is a rather gaudy dry drinking trough, commemorating General Sir Thomas Myddelton Biddulph KCB.

> **WHERE TO EAT AND DRINK** ⓘ
> The café at **Balmoral Castle** serves Queen's teas and a pretty good quiche. The nearby **Inver Hotel** offers bar meals (dogs welcome). Ballater has a selection of fine eating places, from the fish and chip shop to the elegant restaurant at the **Deeside Hotel**.

Turn down the road to the shop in **Easter Balmoral**. You can turn left to revisit the castle, as the route is about to leave the estate by turning right across a stream and down left to a public road alongside the **Dee**.

Turn right, then left, to a white suspension bridge across the river. Follow the road ahead, until a side road on the left leads to **Crathie cemetery**. Here are 17th-century tombs with death's heads and epitaphs, and the grave of Queen Victoria's special friend, the ghillie John Brown. Interest in Brown has been increased by the film *Mrs Brown* starring Billy Connolly and Judi Dench. Brown's grave was inscribed by his Queen 'that friend on whose fidelity you count, that friend given you by circumstances beyond your control, was God's own gift.' It lies midway between the ruined chapel and the south wall of the kirkyard.

The side road continues to the information centre at the end of the car park.

Crombie Water and the Whisky Hills

A walk through a green valley and bare heather moor in the smugglers'
country of Glenlivet.

•DISTANCE•	6¼ miles (10.1km)
•MINIMUM TIME•	3hrs 15min
•ASCENT / GRADIENT•	1,000ft (305m) ▲▲▲
•LEVEL OF DIFFICULTY•	👤👤 👤👤 👤👤
•PATHS•	Waymarked, muddy and indistinct in places, 11 stiles
•LANDSCAPE•	Birchwoods, heather, rolling hills
•SUGGESTED MAP•	aqua3 OS Explorer 420 Correen Hills & Glenlivet
•START / FINISH•	Grid reference: NJ 218257
•DOG FRIENDLINESS•	On leads except in plantation
•PARKING•	Track opposite church at Tombae runs up to quarry car park
•PUBLIC TOILETS•	None on route or near by
•NOTE•	Grouse shooting in August/September – consult Glenlivet Ranger Service at Tomintoul

BACKGROUND TO THE WALK

Long before the coming of licensed distilleries, whisky was part of the economy of the Highlands. After the hard work of the barley harvest came the quieter occupation of mashing and distilling. The draff (dregs) from the mash-barrel went to feed the cows, while the spirit itself warmed the crofter through the snows of winter.

As rents came to be paid in money rather than in kind, whisky was an easily transported product for cash. It was also convenient to tax, but this simply meant that the Highlanders moved their operation into the hills. The barley fields of Strathspey, the clear mountain water of the Cairngorms and the convenient smuggling routes to Aberdeen and Inverness made Glenlivet a famous whisky country. Even as his redcoats were hunting the smugglers through the Ladder Hills, King George IV was demanding the illicit Glenlivet by name.

Water, Malt – and Mystery

The old word 'Scotch' is only applied to whisky – the people are 'Scottish' and the language is 'Scots'. And whiskey with an 'e' comes from Ireland or the United States. Barley is the start-point. The grain is allowed to germinate in the warm, damp environment of the malting floor, which converts some of its starch to sugar. The malt is heated, under the pagoda-like copper roof of the malting kiln, then boiled and fermented into the 'mash', a kind of sweet insipid beer.

The mash is passed three times through the onion-shaped copper stills and stored in barrels for at least eight years. That's the technical process; the added mystery happens almost by accident. The killing of the malt, traditionally done over a peat fire, adds a smoky aroma, but it's the second-hand sherry barrels used for storage that add the golden colour, much of the flavour and the bite of the oakwood.

Blended whiskies, such as Bells, Teachers and Famous Grouse, are made of cheaper corn spirit with malt whisky mixed in. More serious are the 'single malts', each a product of a named distillery. From Glenlivet comes the Glenlivet itself, and also Tomnavoulin, Tomintoul, Cragganmore and Glenfarclas. These are Speyside malts – smooth and subtle. From the islands of the west come wilder whiskies like Lagavoulin and Talisker, with overtones of peat, seaweed and even old fish crates. An educational tasting session could start in the hotels and whisky shops of Tomintoul.

Walk 26 Directions

① At **Tombae church**, turn left for 330yds (300m) to a stile on the right – signposted as Walk 10. A track leads down into birchwoods. Bear right at a waymark and follow the main track to a bridge over the **River Livet**. After another 60yds (55m), turn right to another bridge,

this time over the **Crombie Water**. Turn half left, up to a stile beside a field gate. The walk now follows the top of the low wooded bank above the Crombie Water to reach a footbridge (grid ref 226245).

② Across the footbridge, a small path runs across a meadow into a wood, slanting up to the right to a green track. Turn right and follow this gently up through the wood, then bend left on to heather moorland. Below the abrupt hill of **The Bochel** the track forks. Keep ahead, with a waymark. The way becomes a peaty path. At the top of the first rise is a stile with a gate alongside. The path, with a waymarker, leads to a gateway in another fence. Don't go through, but turn right, with the fence on your left, to a stile with a signpost.

> **WHILE YOU'RE THERE** ⓘ
> **Glenlivet** was the first legal distillery in Scotland. Mechanisation and even computerisation have overtaken the ancient mysteries, but the smell remains the same. Look out for the small dent in one of the copper stills. The result of an unknown accident, it has to be carefully reproduced every time the still gets rebuilt – just in case it may be affecting the whisky.

③ For an easier alternative, follow the sign for Walk 10, ahead. Just before a house, turn right at another signpost and follow a rough track towards Bochel farm. But the main route goes over The Bochel itself. Across the stile, turn uphill on small sheep paths to the summit cairn. Turn left, to descend towards the large white Braeval distillery below the **Ladder Hills**. As the slope steepens, you'll see **Bochel**

> **WHAT TO LOOK FOR** ⓘ
> From the summit of The Bochel, you can see two of Glenlivet's six **distilleries**. In the north, the Tomnavoulin distillery makes a distinguished Speyside malt. Southwards, the white block of **Braeval**, currently not operating, used to contribute to blended whiskies. Behind it, faint green lines slanting up the Ladder Hills are the traces of smugglers paths, where the illicit spirit was carried over to Donside.

> **WHERE TO EAT AND DRINK** ⓘ
> At Tomintoul, the highest village in the Highlands, the air is fresh and scented with whisky. The **Gordon Hotel**'s Cromdale Restaurant serves traditional Scottish food, and bar meals in the Grouse's Nest (dogs and children welcome). Closest to the walk is the **Pole Inn** at Knockandhu, but it's currently on the market.

farm below. Head down the left-hand edge of the nearer pine wood to join the rough track leading into the farm.

④ At once a stile on the right leads to a faint path into the plantation. This soon becomes a green track running just above the bottom edge of the wood. It becomes more well-used and eventually runs out to a road.

⑤ Turn right, over a bridge to a waymarked stile on the right. A track rises to open fields above the river. At its highest point, a waymarker points down to the right. Go down to a fence, with a waymarked stile on the left, then through heather with a fence on your left. Turn downhill to a stile at the bottom. Cross this and turn left, ignoring another stile on the left, to reach the footbridge, Point ②. Retrace the first part of the walk back to **Tombae**.

Loch an Eilein's Castle and Ord Ban

The castle on the island in the loch is the heart of Rothiemurchus Forest.

•DISTANCE•	4¼ miles (6.8km)
•MINIMUM TIME•	1hr 45min
•ASCENT / GRADIENT•	100ft (30m)
•LEVEL OF DIFFICULTY•	
•PATHS•	Wide smooth paths, optional steep hill with high ladder stile
•LANDSCAPE•	Ancient pine forest around loch
•SUGGESTED MAP•	aqua3 OS Explorer 403 Cairn Gorm & Aviemore
•START / FINISH•	Grid reference: NH 897084
•DOG FRIENDLINESS•	On leads on Rothiemurchus Estate
•PARKING•	Estate car park near Loch an Eilein
•PUBLIC TOILETS•	Visitor centre

BACKGROUND TO THE WALK

An island castle, surrounded by ancient pines, and the mountains rising behind – you hardly have to bother with the rest of Scotland, Loch an Eilein has it all.

Castle for Cattle Thieves

Loch an Eilein Castle was built by John Comyn II, known as the Red Comyn, in the 13th century. It guards the strategic cattle-stealing route, the Rathad nam Meirleach, which runs along the shore of the loch. Locals used to keep a cow tied to a tree in hope that the raiders would take that and leave the rest alone. The three murderers of a Macintosh chieftain were imprisoned in chains here for seven years, before being executed in 1531. The castle was most recently fought over in 1690. Grizzel Mhor (Big Grizelda), the chieftain's wife, held it for Clan Grant against the King in 1690. There is said to be an underwater zig-zag causeway leading out to the island.

Life in the Pines

Walk quietly with binoculars and you may see some of the unique birdlife of the forest. The crested tit resembles the more familiar coal tit, with brown body and striped head, but with the Mohican hair-style effect of its crest. It nests in holes in old, rotten trees, so will only be found in wild forest. The Scottish crossbill, found only in Scotland, has a parrot-like beak, adapted for cracking open pine cones. The capercaillie is the large grouse of the forest and its name means 'horse of the woods'. The male challenges and intimidates other males with a noise like the clip-clop of hooves, or like a wine-bottle being opened. Your only real chance of seeing it in the wild is at dawn, in spring, at the RSPB reserve at Loch Garten (better known for its ospreys).

Osprey Island

Ospreys used to nest in the castle ruins. An egg collector once swam across wearing nothing but his cap, which he used to bring back his plunder. Ospreys are back in the Cairngorms, and though they won't return to this over-public island, you might see them elsewhere plunging feet-first as they strike for a trout. Try the trout farm at Inverdruie, on the edge of Aviemore. Sadly, the egg-collectors are back as well. In 2000, a man in Leicester was caught with three stolen osprey eggs.

Romantic Setting

In the romantic novel *The Key above the Door* by Maurice Walsh (1926), the hero and heroine spend half the book gazing at each other from cottages on opposite sides of Loch an Eilein before accidentally getting shipwrecked on the island. More recently, Archie and Katrina, from the popular TV series *Monarch of the Glen*, enjoyed their own romantic encounter on the island.

Walk 27 Directions

① From the end of the car park at the beginning of the walk, a made-up path leads to the visitor centre. Turn left to cross the end of **Loch an Eilein**, then turn right on a smooth sandy track. The loch shore is near by on the right. There are small paths leading down to it if you wish to visit. Just past a red-roofed house, a deer fence runs across, with a gate.

Walk 27

② The track now becomes a wide, smooth path, which runs close to the loch side. After a bridge, the main track forks right to pass a bench backed by a flat boulder. The smaller path on the left leads high into the hills and through the famous pass of the **Lairig Ghru**, eventually to Braemar. After crossing a stream at a low concrete footbridge, the path bends right for 120yds (110m) to a junction. Just beyond is a footbridge with wooden handrails.

WHAT TO LOOK FOR ⓘ

At the foot of the loch, you walk across a low **loggers' dam**. Timber men used to release the water to carry the tree trunks down to the Spey. We usually think of the log-rafts of the great Canadian rivers, but the skill was carried there by Highlanders from Rothiemurchus.

---

③ To shorten the walk, cross this footbridge and continue along the main track, passing Point ④ in another 170yds (155m). For a longer walk, turn left before the footbridge on to a narrower path that will pass around **Loch Gamhna**. This second loch soon appears on your right-hand side. Where the path forks, keep right to pass along the loch side, across its head (rather boggy) and back along its further side, to rejoin the wider path around **Loch an Eilein**. Turn left here.

④ Continue around Loch an Eilein, with the water on your right, to a reedy corner of the loch and a bench. About 55yds (51m) further, the path turns sharply right, signposted 'footpath'. After a gate, turn right to the loch side and a **memorial** to Major General Brook Rice who drowned here while skating. Follow the shore to the point opposite the castle, then back up to the wide track above. A deer fence on the left leads back to the visitor centre.

⑤ From here, a stiff climb (around 500ft/152m) can be made on to the rocky little hill of **Ord Ban**, a superb viewpoint. Cross a ladder stile immediately to the right of the toilet block and follow the deer fence to the right for 150yds (137m), to a point behind the car park. Just behind one of the lowest birches on the slope, a small path zig-zags up the steep slope. It slants to the left to avoid crags, then crosses a small rock slab (take care if wet) and continues on to the summit. Descend by the same path.

WHERE TO EAT AND DRINK ⓘ

Smiffy's Fish & Chips at Aviemore is celebrated across Scotland by hungry hillwalkers and climbers. For even hungrier ones, **La Taverna** offers a pizza and salad 'eat as much as you can' buffet, as well as more formal Italian restaurant fare. You can find it at the south end of Aviemore, opposite the turn-off to Glenmore.

WHILE YOU'RE THERE ⓘ

Careful observers might see the wildcat, pine marten and capercaillie, but it's several centuries too late to spot the extinct wolf, bison and lynx. However, all these can be seen at the **Highland Wildlife Park** at Kincraig. It's an outpost of Edinburgh zoo, where all the Cairngorms' wildlife past and present is kept under fairly natural conditions.

Walk 28

The Pass of Ryvoan and the Thieves' Road

Following cattle thieves and drovers to the lochan used by the fairies for their laundry.

•DISTANCE•	5 miles (8km)
•MINIMUM TIME•	2hrs 15min
•ASCENT / GRADIENT•	400ft (122m) ▲▲▲
•LEVEL OF DIFFICULTY•	🚶 🚶 🚶
•PATHS•	Smooth tracks, one steep ascent, no stiles
•LANDSCAPE•	Views over Rothiemurchus Forest to Cairngorms
•SUGGESTED MAP•	aqua3 OS Explorer 403 Cairn Gorm & Aviemore
•START / FINISH•	Grid reference: NH 980095
•DOG FRIENDLINESS•	Off leads but under close control
•PARKING•	Bridge just south of Glenmore village
•PUBLIC TOILETS•	Glenmore village

BACKGROUND TO THE WALK

The Pass of Ryvoan has all the atmosphere of a classic Cairngorm through-route. It's a scaled down version of the famous and fearsome Lairig Ghru that cuts through the Cairngorm range southwards from Aviemore. You pass from the shelter of the forest to a green lochan, trapped between two high and stony mountainsides. Once through the narrow gap, you're in a different country. Here you will find wide moors and a ring of peaks around the horizon.

Thieving Ways
Ryvoan marked the exit of the Thieves' Road that ran out of Rannoch and Lochaber by secret ways through the Rothiemurchus Forest. The MacDonalds of Glen Coe used to come raiding here in the 17th century, as did Clan Cameron from Loch Eil near Fort William. Once through the pass, they could take their pick from the rich lands of Moray and Aberdeenshire.

In more settled times, the raiding chieftains became landlords, and their rents were paid in the small black cattle of the glens. Every autumn, the drove herds assembled for their long walk to the markets of Falkirk, Perth and northern England.

The Old Drove Road
The drovers used the same road as their thieving grandfathers, but once through the pass they turned sharp right across the flank of the mountain. The Lairig an Lui, the Pass of the Calves, crosses the dangerous ford of the Avon and runs down Glen Derry to Braemar. It's 30 miles (48km) to the next good grazing and shelter from the rain – two full days for the drove. Overnight the cattle would snatch some grazing from the rough grasses, while the drovers cooked their oatmeal and potatoes, before rolling themselves in their woollen plaids on a bed of heather. As late as 1859, Queen Victoria found the Lairig path torn up by hooves and scented with fresh cow pats.

The Sith and Others

Lochan Uaine means 'Green Loch'. Some say the green colour is caused by flecks of mica. Others claim that it's where the fairies wash their green garments. The Highland fairies, the Sith (pronounced 'Shee'), don't dance around with magic wands and grant you three wishes. They are touchy and vengeful, and if you meet one it is best to address him very politely in good Gaelic. Precautions you can take are to avoid wearing green, which is known to annoy them, and never to address your friends by name while still under the trees.

The Bodach Lamh-dearg is a spectre who appears wrapped in a grey plaid with one bloodstained hand, challenging passers-by to a fight and leaving their bodies for the foxes. Big Donald, the King of the Fairies, lived beside Loch Morlich. While wolves and bears may one day return to the forest, we should be more alarmed about the return of the Sith.

Walk 28 Directions

① Head upstream on a sandy track to the left of the river. Interpretation signs explain the flowers of the forest you may come

across, many of which are ferns and mosses. After 550yds (503m), turn left on a wide smooth path with blue/yellow waymarkers. Ahead is a gate into **Glenmore Lodge** rifle range; here the path bends right, to a wide gravel track.

② Turn right, away from Glenmore Lodge, to cross a concrete bridge into the **Caledonian Reserve**. Immediately keep ahead on a smaller track (marked by a blue waymarker) as the main one bends right. The track narrows as it heads into the **Pass of Ryvoan** between steep wooded slopes of pine, birch and scree. At a sign that warns of the end of waymarking, a path turns left, with a blue waymarker, which you take in a moment. Just beyond this, steps on the right lead down to **Lochan Uaine**. Walk round to left of the water on the beach. At the head of the loch a small path leads back up to the track. Turn sharp left, back to the junction already visited; now turn off to the right on to the narrower path with the blue waymarker.

③ This small path crosses some duckboard and heads back down the valley. Very soon it starts to climb steeply to the right, up rough stone steps. When it levels off the going is easier, although it's still narrow with tree roots. The path reaches a forest road at a bench and a waymarker.

WHERE TO EAT AND DRINK

The Forestry Commission's **visitor centre** has a café serving baked potatoes and snacks. Across the road, the **Glenmore Café** offers chips, toasties and red squirrels – the squirrels are outside, using a feeder placed directly opposite the windows.

---

④ Continue to the left along the track. After a clear-felled area with views, the track re-enters trees and slopes downhill into Glenmore village. Just above the main road turn right, through a green barrier, to reach **Glenmore Visitor Centre**. Pass through its car park to the main road.

WHILE YOU'RE THERE

Reintroduced to the Cairngorms after an absence of around 1,000 years, the Glenmore **reindeer** herd is based at Glenmore village. From the Reindeer Centre you'll be taken up the hill to visit the herd. Some of the reindeer pull sleighs in Christmas parades in December, and all are tame enough to handle.

---

⑤ Cross to **Glenmore shop** with its café. Behind a red post-box, steps lead down to the campsite. Pass along its right-hand edge to a wide smooth path into birch woods (blue/brown waymarkers). Head left across a footbridge to the shore of **Loch Morlich** and follow the shore's sandy beaches (or paths in the woods on the left) until another river blocks the way. Turn left along the riverbank. Ignore a footbridge, but continue on the wide path (following brown/blue waymarkers) with the river on your right. Where the path divides, the smaller branch, with blue waymarkers, continues beside the river through broom bushes to the car park at the start of the walk.

WHAT TO LOOK FOR

Elsewhere in Britain, **red squirrels** are being supplanted by their big grey cousins which were introduced from America. However, the red squirrel's smaller teeth are better adapted to life among the pines, and it is widespread in the Rothiemurchus Forest. Typically they'll run up the side of a tree trunk facing away from you, but then you'll see them escaping through the branches overhead. Close up – as at the Glenmore Café – you may notice their vicious little claws and teeth and realise they're nothing more than fluffy orange rats.

Meall a' Bhuachaille

Looking at the Cairngorms from a smallish mountain above the fairy lochan.
See map and information panel for Walk 28

•DISTANCE•	6½ miles (10.4km)
•MINIMUM TIME•	4hrs
•ASCENT / GRADIENT•	1,700ft (518m) ▲▲▲
•LEVEL OF DIFFICULTY•	🚶🚶🚶

Walk 29 Directions (Walk 28 option)

Leaving the summit of Meall a' Bhuachaille in mist is tricky, so inexperienced walkers should only attempt this walk in clear weather.

Walk 28 leads to the sign 'End of Waymarking' (Point ③) and **Lochan Uaine**. From the loch head (Point Ⓐ), turn right along the track to continue up the valley. The gable of **Ryvoan bothy** (shepherd's hut) is briefly visible ahead. The track forks; turn left, signed 'Nethy Bridge', to the bothy (Point Ⓑ).

Here a path turns off to the left, to climb **Meall a' Bhuachaille**. It soon becomes steep and stony, eases off slightly, then steepens again. Once above these you can no longer look back down on the bothy. The path here is gentler, but peaty and soggy. As the ground becomes stony again, the path branches, with the right-hand one giving views down into Strath Nethy.

In the pass below, pines from the north and the south are about to rejoin. Soon squirrels will hop, branch to branch, from Grantown to Glen Feshie.

The paths rejoin to reach a cairn, with the summit about 550yds (500m) beyond. Here you will find a large cairn (Point Ⓒ), with a circular shelter of low stones. Note that you arrive from the direction of the opening in this shelter.

To leave the summit, turn right to pass a smaller cairn a few steps away. The path is unclear at first, becoming wider. The slope eases and becomes boggy. Here the main path turns down to the left (Point Ⓓ: ignore a smaller path running ahead to the col just below).

Follow this main path down off the ridge – it is wide and peaty, with a rebuilt section and then more peat, as it slants around **Coire Chondlaich**. Maps show this path as following the stream down, but in fact it heads out to the right, reaching the top of the trees about 300yds (274m) to the right of the stream. Here an orange-topped post (Point Ⓔ) marks the top of a wide smooth path.

The path bends left to a footbridge, then turns downhill with the stream on its right. At a fork, a smaller path on the right has the orange waymarker, and soon arrives at **Glenmore** village (Point ⑤ of Walk 28).

Boat of Garten and the Spey

Along the banks of the great river, with a pinewood return.

•DISTANCE•	5¾ miles (9.2km)
•MINIMUM TIME•	2hrs 15min
•ASCENT / GRADIENT•	197ft (60m)
•LEVEL OF DIFFICULTY•	
•PATHS•	Riverside path, wide woodland track, no stiles
•LANDSCAPE•	Wide River Spey, pine forest
•SUGGESTED MAP•	aqua3 OS Explorer 403 Cairn Gorm & Aviemore
•START / FINISH•	Grid reference: NH 945191
•DOG FRIENDLINESS•	Dogs not welcome on riverside – use track on right
•PARKING•	Small pull-in at east of Boat of Garten village, next to bridge
•PUBLIC TOILETS•	Boat of Garten

Walk 30 Directions

You can walk out on to Garten Bridge for the upstream view, but return to the same end. Villages with the name 'Boat' are the sites of former ferries. The 1974 concrete bridge replaced a wooden bridge of 1899, which itself replaced the boat. The Osprey Bar has a picture of the chain ferry and the newly built bridge above it.

At the village end of the bridge, on the upstream side, a small kissing gate is marked 'No Dogs'. It leads to a riverside path upstream. The path, one tree back from the river so it doesn't disturb the fish and the anglers, runs through a wood, where monkey flower is bright yellow in the ditches, and past a beach of golden sand. Rest a while at one of the benches and you might see a kingfisher. The path now runs along the edge of the riverside field, with views ahead to the high Cairngorms. Giant knapweeds grow here, thistle-like but without the prickles.

The Spey is one of the great rivers of Scotland. It wanders across its wide strath (mountain valley) in great meanders, in the style of a mature river. In fact it's still 650ft (198m) above sea level. At times of storm or snow-melt it became impassible, and it was only after it was bridged, during the early 19th century, that northern Scotland became fully accessible.

For centuries before that, the river was itself a highway for the floaters – the men who brought the logs down out of the forests of the Cairngorms. Today, canoeists, much to the annoyance of the salmon fishers, have established their own right of navigation in the river. The riverside path continues through pastureland with gorse. A house blocks the riverside ahead; turn right, at a waymarker and sign, 'Kinveachy Road', and cross a field to a track. Turn left along the track. It runs parallel to the river, which is near by on the left, then bends right, into a wood of birches and broom. Where it bends left, a path ahead (again signed 'Kinveachy

Road') could be used to shorten the walk drastically. The main route keeps on along the track. It rejoins the river at a deep reach of smooth water, and runs through meadows. With the **fishing lodge** of Kinchurdy ahead, a gate leads out on to a wider, stony track.

> ### WHERE TO EAT AND DRINK
> The **Boat Hotel**, in Boat of Garten, is the original station hotel, once popular with Victorian sportsmen. Its Osprey Bar and Capercaillie Restaurant serve fresh game and salmon, also haggis. It's so popular that you usually need to book. No dogs, but children are welcome.

Turn right, away from the river. On the left is **Loch Dallas**, where mallard and other ducks can often be seen. Follow the track for a mile (1.6km), passing a dead birch tree with many bracket fungus growing on it. The **Speyside Way** joins from the left and, immediately afterwards, the track passes under the granite bridge of the Speyside steam railway.

The Speyside Way, Scotland's third long distance path, has finally become continuous from Aviemore to the sea at Spey Bay, and an extension is planned upriver to Newtonmore. It uses the former Spey railway, closed by Dr Beeching in the 1960s, for much of its length. It's a smooth and level walk, where the main difficulty may be in negotiating the various distilleries alongside the route.

Here, however, the Way has been evicted from its track by the Speyside Steam Railway, reopened for tourists. It now runs through Bridge of Garten to Broomhill, whose station is Glen Bogle in the TV series *Monarch of the Glen*.

Once under the bridge the main track bends right, signed 'Kinveachy Road'; instead turn half-right on a green track that veers to the left. On the right is **Geordie's Yard**, with an interesting collection of old bicycles. Ahead a gate leads into pine woods. Walk round it and continue for 50yds (46m), turning right at a sign, 'Woodland Walks'.

An earth track leads through pine and heather. Once more you're in the regenerating **Caledonian Forest**. This is described as semi-wild: it was planted fairly recently, but is now being allowed to regenerate of its own accord. Thickets of young trees are thinning themselves by natural wastage, gradually creating a more open style of woodland.

The track passes two more signposts, where you stay on the main track ahead. At the edge of the village, turn right signed 'Woodland Walks', and left at the corner of a football pitch. Near **Boat of Garten**'s main street, a further Woodland Walks signpost points to the right, to another junction. (Here a right turn leads to the **Fairy Hill** viewpoint in the forest, ¼ mile/400m away.) The path on the left leads between houses to the village street. Turn right and follow it round two bends to **Garten Bridge** and the start point.

> ### WHAT TO LOOK FOR
> On the left as you approach Boat of Garten is an area of **fire damaged forest**. Heather and pine are the only plants resinous enough to burn while still alive and growing. The fire here has blackened the trunks and consumed the heather undergrowth, with bilberry now growing in its place, but the trees have survived, losing only their lower branches.

Looking over the Sea to Skye

A coast walk along Loch Alsh with views of Skye, the sea and a fish farm.

Walk 31

•DISTANCE•	7¼ miles (11.7km)
•MINIMUM TIME•	3hrs 30min
•ASCENT / GRADIENT•	750ft (228m) ▲▲▲
•LEVEL OF DIFFICULTY•	林 林 林
•PATHS•	Tracks, grassy shoreline, minor road, no stiles
•LANDSCAPE•	Wooded coast, moorland pass
•SUGGESTED MAP•	aqua3 OS Explorer 413 Knoydart, Loch Hourn & Loch Duich
•START / FINISH•	Grid reference: NG 795213
•DOG FRIENDLINESS•	Off lead most of walk
•PARKING•	Above pier of Glenelg ferry
•PUBLIC TOILETS•	None on route or near by

BACKGROUND TO THE WALK

Two hundred years ago, Scotland's rivers were full of salmon, and smoked salmon was the crofter's winter food store. When wild salmon became scarce it was considered a luxury food, and today, if you buy salmon, it's almost certainly from a farm like those you will see on this walk.

Fish Farming

A fish farm should be sheltered from storm waves, but in water at least 30ft (10m) deep so that fish droppings don't poison the fish. There should be a vigorous tidal flow to carry oxygen-rich water into the pens, no pollution and the water should be cool, but should not freeze. In other words, it should be in a Scottish sea loch. Scotland's 340 farms are valued at £260m, they employ 6,500 people and produce 120,000 tonnes of fish a year, enough to give every Briton a 4oz (100g) steak twice a month.

Fish farming is a tough life. Mending a net that's 3ft (90cm) underwater is not comfortable when the water is still, but it invariably isn't, because the day when it's blowing half a gale is the very day the nets break. Hauling the cages out of the water for cleaning is the toughest job of all – seaweed grows on fish farms just as it does on the shoreline, and after two years it starts to hinder the flow of water. And a single storm, or even a passing whale, can tear the nets and lose the work of two years.

Mass Catering

During its first 40 years, fish farming, like farming on land, has tried to produce as much as possible, as cheaply as possible. Salmon are stocked like battery hens and fed a high-fat diet. Antibiotics keep them alive if not altogether healthy, and dyes give their flesh the pink colour. One result has been pollution from their droppings poisoning nearby shellfish beds. Fish farms act as reservoirs of disease, in particular of the parasitic sea-lice. There are many reasons for the decline of the wild salmon and infection from fish farms is one of them.

Scottish fish farming has now reached the point where it has to clean up its act. A recent development is the organic fish farm, where the fish are stocked less densely and are fed a more natural diet. Fish pens are circular because the salmon prefer to swim round and round. If they were put in a square enclosure, the corners would be wasted. More importantly, the fish would hit the sides four times as they went round, and this would damage their scales.

Walk 31 Directions

① A track runs out of the car park, signed for Ardintoul and Totaig. It ascends gently through two gates,

then goes through a third into a plantation. With high power lines just above, the track forks. Take the left-hand one, downhill, passing an arrow painted on a rock. The track runs between the feet of a tall pylon

WHILE YOU'RE THERE ⓘ
In Glenelg village, **Bernera Barracks**, now an imposing but dangerous ruin, is one of the forts used to pacify Scotland after the 1715 rising (▶ Walk 22). South of the village, the two **Glenelg brochs**, Dun Telve and Dun Troddan, are the finest on the mainland. These impressive stone towers, standing about half their original height, were probably built as emergency shelters against Viking raids.

and then climbs again to contour through a birch wood. It runs in and out of a tiny stream gorge, then gently descends towards the shore. On the other side of **Loch Alsh**, the white houses of **Balmacara** are directly ahead.

③ At the shoreline, the track disappears into an open field strip. Follow the short-cropped grass next to the shingle beach, passing a salmon farm just offshore. When the trees once more run down to the sea, a green track runs next to the shore. It passes below a small crag with birches to reach open flat ground near **Ardintoul Farm**. Keep along the shore, outside field walls, and sometimes taking to the stripy schist shingle, towards a square brick building on the point ahead. Before reaching it you come to a wall gap. Here a track that's simply

WHAT TO LOOK FOR ⓘ
The straits of Kyle Akin and Kyle Rhea are named after two legendary giants who used to leap across the narrows using their spears. Today's equivalent of the pole-vaulting giant is the mighty, double-size **pylon** that carries the power line to Skye. Your path actually passes between its toes. The L12 pylon was designed by Gilbert Scott, architect of Liverpool Cathedral and the red phone box, as a magnificent and sculptural symbol of the bright new age of the 1950s.

a pair of green ruts runs directly inland. It joins a gravel track, where you turn left to pass sheds and a house to regain the shoreline at **Ardintoul**.

③ The track runs along the shoreline, then turns inland to climb the hill behind. The steeper uphill sections are tarred. Below on the left, the **Allt na Dalach** runs into **Loch Alsh**, with a beautifully clear example of a gravel spit where river debris runs into tidal water. The track enters plantations, crosses a stream and bends right to complete its climb to the **Bealach Luachrach**. Here you may see fresh peat workings on the left.

WHERE TO EAT AND DRINK ⓘ
The long-established **Glenelg Inn** offers fine Scottish food in its restaurant, with local seafood a speciality; also bar lunches and suppers (children and dogs welcome). In the bar you'll hear pipe music rather than piped music, and otters can sometimes be seen on the shoreline rocks just outside.

④ The energetic can make a diversion here on to **Glas Bheinn** – a tough little hill, but a fine viewpoint. The grading and timing given for this walk don't take account of this side-trip. From the road's high point, turn right up a wet tree gap to reach open hillside. Follow the remains of an old fence up the first rise. Where it bends right, continue straight uphill to the summit, returning by the same route. The old fence makes a useful guide back into the tree gap. Continue downhill from Point ④ on the unsurfaced road, which reaches the tarred public road a mile (1.6km) north of **Glenelg** village. A grassy verge between road and sea leads back to the ferry pier.

Heart of the Cuillins

Classic rock climbing country below the Cioch and the Inaccessible Pinnacle.

•DISTANCE•	5¾ miles (9.2km)
•MINIMUM TIME•	4hrs
•ASCENT / GRADIENT•	1,900ft (580m) ▲▲▲
•LEVEL OF DIFFICULTY•	🚶 🚶 🚶
•PATHS•	Mountain paths, one boggy and tough, 2 stiles
•LANDSCAPE•	Peaty slopes into spectacular crag hollow
•SUGGESTED MAP•	aqua3 OS Explorer 411 Skye – Cuillin Hills
•START / FINISH•	Grid reference: NG 409206
•DOG FRIENDLINESS•	Signs indicate on leads in sheep country below corrie
•PARKING•	Walkers' pull-off before gate into Glenbrittle campsite
•PUBLIC TOILETS•	At campsite

BACKGROUND TO THE WALK

The Black Cuillin Hills, seen through Skye's moist Atlantic air, appear blue and under romantic sunset light almost purple. This land is like nowhere else, even in Scotland, for crag, boulder and jagged horizon.

The Glory of Gabbro

The special quality of Skye is obvious to the eye, but even more so to the foot. The black rock grips the foot like velcro. This is gabbro, formed in the magma chamber of a volcano bigger than Kilimanjaro that stood here 50 million years ago. Skye's screes are the steepest, its crags the craggiest, and its ridges look out across the Hebrides and the Atlantic. For rock climbers and mountaineers, on the rare days when it isn't raining, this is paradise.

As you approach Point ④ on the upward journey, you are looking towards the buttress of Sron na Ciche. High on the face is a smooth, diamond-shaped slab and, at its right-hand corner, a famous rock-projection. It long went unnoticed, until a famous climber, Professor Norman Collie, spotted the shadow it casts across the slab in the afternoon. This is A'Chioch, 'the Breast'. Its flat top was the scene of a sword-fight in the film *Highlander*. The top is reached by a spectacular, but fairly straightforward climb.

Behind Lagan

In the upper corrie, more famous bits of rock come into view. At the back right corner is the long scree called the Great Stone Shoot. It is strenuous and frustrating but not technically difficult, and it brings climbers up to the ridge just to the right of Skye's highest peak, Sgurr Alasdair. The skyline to left of the Stone Shoot is dominated by Sgurr Mhic Choinnich, with its near-vertical right profile. This step, 200ft (61m) high, can be avoided by a remarkable ledge that crosses below the summit, to emerge on the mountain's gentler left-hand ridge.

To the left again, you can just see the rock-prow of the so-called Inaccessible Pinnacle. This forms the summit of Skye's second highest peak, Sgurr Dearg. Its easiest route is very scary, but only moderately difficult and not particularly inaccessible. It must be climbed by anyone wishing to complete the Munro summits, Scottish peaks over 3,000ft (914m), and on summer weekends there will be a queue of several hours at its foot.

0 ½ Mile

0 ½ Km

Sgurr Alasdair

948 ▲

▲ 993

Sgurr Mhic
Choinnich

Great Stone Shoot

▲ 947

▲ 859

⑤

A' Chioch

986 ▲

Sgurr Dearg

Sron na
Ciche

④ COIRE
LAGAN

Allt Coire Lagan

LOCH AN FHIR-
BHALLAICH

▲ 288

—Z—

ALLT COIRE NA BANACHDICH

EAS MOR

③

Culnamean

WC

② shop

Carbost

① P

MEMORIAL
HUT

GLENBRITTLE
CAMPSITE

Loch Brittle

Walk 32 Directions

① From the parking area, the track leads on through **Glenbrittle campsite** to a gate with a kissing gate. Pass to left of the toilet block to cross a stile. Turn left along a stony track just above, which runs gently downhill above the campsite, to rejoin the **Glenbrittle road**.

WHAT TO LOOK FOR ℹ️

After the gabbro formed, molten **basalt** was forced sideways into any cracks. The picnic rocks at the outflow of Loch Coire Lagan are crossed by **basalt dykes**, about 1ft (30cm) wide. The basalt is the same black colour as the gabbro around it, but smooth and blocky in texture. Basalt breaks up easily, and its dykes form the cracks and narrow gullies that run up and down the rock faces. The typical Cuillin skyline is notched with basalt dykes.

---

② Keep ahead to cross a bridge with the white **Memorial Hut** just ahead. On the right are some stone buchts (sheep-handling enclosures) and here a waymarked path heads uphill to reach a footbridge over the **Allt Coire na Banachdich**.

③ Cross the footbridge and head up to the right of the stream's deep ravine. Look out for a short side-path on the left for the best view of the waterfall at its head. Its Gaelic name, **Eas Mor**, means simply 'Big Waterfall'. Above, the path bears right, to slant up the hillside. This part of the path has never been built or repaired and is bog and boulder. It passes above **Loch an Fhir-bhallaich** and forks, with the left-hand and higher branch being drier but with loose eroded scree. It rounds a shoulder into the lower part of **Coire Lagan** and meets a much larger and better path.

④ Turn uphill on this path, until a belt of bare rock blocks the way into the upper corrie. This rock has been smoothed by a glacier into gently-rounded swells, known as 'boiler-plates'. A scree field runs up into the boiler-plate rocks. The best way keeps up the left edge, below a slab wall with a small waterslide, to the highest point of the scree. Head up left for a few steps on bare rock, then back right on ledges to an eroded scree above the boiler-plate obstruction. Look back down your upward route to note it for your return. The trodden way slants up to the right. With the main stream near by on the right, it goes up to the rim of the upper corrie.

WHERE TO EAT AND DRINK ℹ️

The **Sligachan Hotel** has been refreshing rock climbers for over a century. The hotel serves the Skye-brewed Black Cuillin beer along with walker-size meals in its barn-like bar. No dogs, but children are welcome.

---

⑤ The boiler-plate slabs at the lochan's outflow are excellent for picnics. Walking mainly on bare rock, it's easy to make a circuit of the lochan. For the return journey, retrace your steps to Point ④. Ignoring the right fork of the route you came up by, keep straight downhill on the main path. It runs straight down to the toilet block at **Glenbrittle campsite**.

WHILE YOU'RE THERE ℹ️

There's an easier way into the heart of the Cuillins. **Loch Coruisk** is a few steps from the sea, but completely shut in by the horseshoe-shaped mountain range. It can be reached by rock climbing, a tough walk or boat, from Elgol. A trip in the *Bella Jane* gives you 1hr 30min or 4hrs 30min ashore returning past the Scavaig seal colony.

Prison and Pinnacle

Exploring the weird lava landscape of Skye's northern peninsula.

•DISTANCE•	5¼ miles (8.4km)
•MINIMUM TIME•	3hrs
•ASCENT / GRADIENT•	1,200ft (365m) ▲▲▲
•LEVEL OF DIFFICULTY•	🚶🚶 🚶🚶 🚶
•PATHS•	Well-used path, 1 stile
•LANDSCAPE•	Rock towers and pinnacles
•SUGGESTED MAP•	aqua3 OS Explorer 408 Skye – Trotternish & the Storr
•START / FINISH•	Grid reference: NG 440679
•DOG FRIENDLINESS•	On leads passing sheep, care on cliff top
•PARKING•	Pull-in, top of pass on Staffin–Uig road. Overflow parking at cemetery ¼ mile (400m) on Staffin side (not available during funerals)
•PUBLIC TOILETS•	Brogaig

BACKGROUND TO THE WALK

The rocks of Scotland vary from ancient – about 400 million years – to a great deal older than that, but along the western edge is something quite different. The great eye of the Atlantic Ocean opened at a time that, geologically speaking, is this morning just before breakfast. A mere 60 million years ago, the mid-Atlantic ridge lay just off the Scottish coast. And all along that ridge, new seabed emerged in exotic and interesting volcanic rocks that now form the Arran granite, the basalt of Mull and Skye, and the Skye gabbro.

Lava Landscape

Stir together butter and sugar in a saucepan, take the mixture off the heat and it crystallises into fudge. But take the same ingredients and cool them quickly, by tipping them into cold water, for example, and you get the glassy solid we call toffee. Now take a basic silicaceous magma, let it cool over thousands of years deep inside a volcano, and you'll get the rough crystalline gabbro that featured on Walk 32. But let it erupt suddenly at the surface, and it congeals into basalt, which is black, shiny and slippery. It forms a completely different sort of scenery – that of northern Skye.

Basalt lava is a slippery liquid, like milk rather than treacle. This makes it quite different from the lumpy rhyolite lava that formed Glen Coe and the craggy side of Ben Nevis. Basalt lava spreads in wide, shallow layers across the country. After erosion, you get a flat-topped landscape, with long low cliffs at the edges and wide grassy plateaux. Macleod's Tables, behind Walk 38, are lava-layer hills, as is Dun Caan on Raasay (► Walk 36).

North of Portree, the lava flowed out over older, softer rocks of Jurassic (dinosaur) age. All along the Trotternish peninsula, the sea has been steadily removing those softer rocks, and the basalt above has been breaking off in hill-sized chunks and slipping downhill and eastwards. The chunks lean over, split apart and erode: the result is some extraordinary scenery, of which the queerest is the Quiraing.

Some of its rock forms, with intriguing names such as the Prison, the Needle and the Fingalian Slab, have been a tourist must-see since Victorian times. As a result, a wide, well-made path leads below these pinnacles, then back along the top. This is good, but for the full tottering splendour of the place, you'll need to follow Walk 34. That steep and rugged way threads among the needles to the heart of the mountain. Here you will find a gently undulating lawn, quite suitable for a spot of croquet, that's called the Table. Spread your picnic cloth on the Table, and then peep out between the rock architecture to the Sound of Raasay and the distant hills of Torridon.

Walk 33 **Directions**

① A well-built path starts at a 'bendy road' sign opposite the lay-by. The jagged tower of grass and

rock on the skyline is the Prison. The path crosses the steep landslip slope towards it, with an awkward crossing of a small stream gully on bare rock, then passes a small waterfall high above and heads to

Walk 33

WHAT TO LOOK FOR

Basalt rock is alkaline and relatively rich in lime and minerals, so its soils support meadow flowers such as would more usually be seen in the English countryside. I have spotted yellow rattle, a flower of ancient pastureland. Sron Vourlinn grows daisies like any suburban lawn. Global warming has encouraged the marbled white butterfly, blotchy brown and white, to move north from England as well.

the right rather than up into a rocky gap. It turns uphill into the wide col to the left of **the Prison**.

② The main path does not drop, but goes forward, slightly uphill, crossing an old fence line at a crag foot. It crosses the foot of steep ground, then passes above a small peat pool. Ignore a path forking down right; the main path slants up left into a col where an old wall runs across.

③ The path descends into a landslip valley that runs across rather than down the hillside, then slants up left to a col with a stile.

④ Cross and turn right for the excursion to **Sron Vourlinn**. Follow the crest over a slightly rocky section with a short descent beyond, then join the main path along a grassy meadow with a very

WHILE YOU'RE THERE

Kilt Rock is seen from a clifftop viewpoint at Staffin. The warning (in Gaelic and five other languages) not to climb over the fence seems scarcely necessary as immediately beyond is a 500ft (152m) drop to the sea. Lean over to see the startling waterfall and columnar basalt cliff. Some of the six-sided blocks have fallen off and lie in the sea directly below the platform.

sudden edge on the right. After the highest point, continue slightly downhill to the north top. Here you can see that the land is still slipping, with a crevasse beside the cliff edge where another narrow section is shortly to peel away. The shelter of the rock crevice grows luxuriant rock rose, rowan and valerian.

⑤ Return to the col with the stile (Point ④) and continue uphill. The drops are now on your left, as you look down towards the pinnacles surrounding the Table. After passing broken ground on the right, you come to a fallen wall, part of which appears from below as a cairn. The path continues next to the cliff edge on the left; you can fork off right, directly uphill, to the summit trig point on **Meall na Suiramach**.

WHERE TO EAT AND DRINK

The Pieces of Ate café at Brogaig lies at the foot of the hill road. It serves home-made snacks and soup from a small shack, but it's closed on Sundays, like most on the island. Magnificently sited below the Quiraing crags, the Flodigarry Hotel offers evening meals and Sunday lunch at its Waterhorse restaurant, specialising in local lobster and other seafood, with bar meals in the public bar (dogs welcome) and conservatory.

⑥ Follow a broad, gentle path slightly downhill to a cairn at the cliff edge. You now look straight down on to **the Table**, 100ft (30m) below. Turn right on the wide path. After a mile (1.6km), the path starts to descend alongside the cliff edge. As the edge turns half right, you should turn fully right. The path is faint, but reappears ahead contouring around the fairly steep grass slope. Once above the car park it turns straight downhill for a final steep descent.

Climbing on the Table

Threading behind the Needle where the MacDonalds hid their cattle.
See map and information panel for Walk 33

•DISTANCE•	5¾ miles (9.2km)
•MINIMUM TIME•	4hrs
•ASCENT / GRADIENT•	1,800ft (548m) ▲▲▲
•LEVEL OF DIFFICULTY•	🚶🚶🚶

Walk 34 Directions
(Walk 33 option)

From Walk 33 you can make a short but strenuous diversion to the Table. This takes you into the heart of the bizarre rock formations above the secret stronghold where the people of Staffin hid their cattle; the name Quiraing means a round cattle enclosure.

A sprawling cairn stands in the col (Point ②), with a jumble of crags and towers above, most noticeably the pointed pinnacle of **the Needle** (Point Ⓐ). An eroded path zig-zags up the steep slope towards it, then up to its left. The path, easier now, turns right to contour behind the Needle, and across the head of a gully of grass and stones.

It then heads into a narrow gap between two rock towers (Point Ⓑ). The gritty passage between the two towers is slightly awkward, and has an extraordinary atmosphere, like a slot canyon or limestone ravine transported to a Hebridean hillside. Even if the raiders could believe this was the way to the cows – and they wouldn't – a single man could defend it against any number.

The path contours forward through a hollow full of pinnacles and then turns uphill. It winds up on grassy terraces among yet more pinnacles and low cliffs.

When the cliff of **Meall na Suiramach** blocks further progress upwards, the wide grass plateau of **the Table** is on the right. Low crags form three of its sides; by passing up and to the right, into the gap behind it, you'll find a path to its flat top (Point Ⓒ). It's a picnic spot with room for several thousand.

Two large rock towers block part of the outward view from the Table. The gap between them has a pencil-shaped pinnacle. This gap is not the way down, but provides the marker for starting the descent. Directly above the pencil pinnacle, a short rocky path drops off the edge of the Table. At the terrace below turn left into a wide gully 50yds (46m) to the left of the pencil pinnacle.

A small path goes down the gully. After 100yds (91m), a tower stands in the gully floor and the path goes down to the right of this. Below the tower it slants steeply down to the left, to join the main Quiraing path, just above a small peat pool (Point Ⓓ). Turn left along Walk 33 for ¼ mile (400m) to Point ③.

Walk 35

Skye and the Sea

A comfortable coastal track above Loch Brittle and on to a former fortified peninsula.

•DISTANCE•	5¼ miles (8.4km)
•MINIMUM TIME•	2hrs 15min
•ASCENT / GRADIENT•	400ft (122m) ▲▲▲
•LEVEL OF DIFFICULTY•	炏 炏 炏
•PATHS•	Track, then well-marked path, 1 stile
•LANDSCAPE•	Rocky moorland and coastline
•SUGGESTED MAP•	aqua3 OS Explorer 411 Skye – Cuillin Hills
•START / FINISH•	Grid reference: NG 409206
•DOG FRIENDLINESS•	On leads
•PARKING•	Walkers' pull-off at gate into Glenbrittle campsite
•PUBLIC TOILETS•	At campsite

Walk 35 Directions

This is an easy coastal walk on good, firm paths. It's popular on days when the mountains are sulking under a cloak of cloud, when hillwalkers would otherwise be attempting the famous Inaccessible Pinnacle up on the ridge. But the views back from Creag Mhor make it just as worthwhile, even on those very special days when you can see the Cuillin Hills.

From the parking area, the track leads on through the campsite to a gate with a kissing gate. The campsite shop, which sells ice cream and midge nets, is just up to the left here. Go through the gate and pass to the left of the campsite's toilet block to cross a stile. Here paths divide; take the right-hand one, below a watertank.

The path runs just above the shoreline and is reasonably clear and firm. After crossing two small streams, it reaches the much larger **Allt Coire Lagan**, which drains the high wild corrie visited in Walk 32.

If the stream is too full to cross, head upstream for a short distance to a footbridge, then continue up to join a track that parallells the path at a slightly higher level. If you do manage to cross the Allt Coire Lagan, the path continues beyond, becoming gradually fainter and bearing up left to join the track just mentioned.

Across **Loch Brittle** is a landscape of flat layers, typical basalt country formed from lava flows. You are crossing similar ground on the walk, very different from the jagged Cuillins above. Soon after you join it, the track reduces to a wide path.

> **WHERE TO EAT AND DRINK** ⓘ
> The **Old Inn** at Carbost has a terrace overlooking Loch Harport. This is a local pub rather than a tourist resort. It has stone walls and bare wooden floors. The bar food is inexpensive and substantial. Dogs and children are welcome.

It fords a stream on bare rock, with a little gorge and waterfall just above. Now the way, while remaining easy, becomes more exciting; a low outcrop is above, and the top edge of sea cliffs are just below the path. At the next stream crossing the path forks. Take the left-hand, upper branch. Cairns mark the way as it ascends gradually, crossing a small stream and reaching the corner of a lochan. This moorland pool, with its bogbean and waterlilies, is a foreground for the Cuillin peaks. From here you're looking straight into Coire Lagan. At the back right corner of the corrie is Sgurr Alasdair, the highest point of Skye.

WHILE YOU'RE THERE ⓘ

If you think the Cuillins are scary, then you certainly shouldn't visit the **Skye Serpentarium** at Broadford. However, you could steer clear of the snake-handling sessions and instead just see the baby tortoises. Still not tempted? They also have lizards, iguanas and tree frogs.

Just beyond the lochan, the path runs up to the small summit of **Creag Mhor**. Ahead and to the left is the island of Soay. Here Gavin Maxwell, author of *Ring of Bright Water*, set up an unsuccessful shark-fishing enterprise. Further away, the Isle of Rum is of the same rugged black rock as the Cuillins.

Looking down to the right, towards Loch Brittle, you can see the return path just below. Ahead, a faultline valley crosses the entire peninsula from side to side. This is the Slochd Dubh, or Black Gap. For thousands of years, the peninsula beyond the Slochd Dubh was a place of settlement and sanctuary, the stronghold of the MacAskills. Only

150 years ago there were still 20 families living here. A small canal has been built to let rowing galleys through at high tide into the small Loch na h-Airde. Above it is a fortified promontory or dun whose stonework still stands. All this ground today is very tough walking, where the small paths peter out into a jumble of bog and crag. Directions for this, if you want them, are simple. Go past the wall that runs along the Slochd Dubh, get lost, then come back to the same point.

Your route goes down to the **Slochd Dubh** and then turns back. From **Creag Mhor** the direct descent into the valley is steep, but there's a grassy gap a few steps away on the left. Don't go through the wall, but bend round to the right, to pass below the outcrop of Creag Mhor, with the sea below on your left. The clear but fairly bouldery path soon rejoins the outward route.

For a slightly easier return to the campsite, keep following the rough track that runs above the path of the outward journey. At the ford of **Allt Coire Lagan**, go down to the footbridge if necessary, then rejoin the track. Once above the campsite, a small path on the left runs down to the toilet block.

WHAT TO LOOK FOR ⓘ

For those who go adventuring beyond Slochd Dubh, there's a neolithic **chambered cairn** at the north end of Loch na h-Airde. A wall runs from the sea to the loch head, with a gap for the path – the cairn is just before the wall, and about 20yds (18m) to left of the gap. Its entrance archway still stands, although its central room has collapsed. Pieces of pottery and six skeletons were found here.

A Raasay Roundabout

Seaside and woodland lead to Raasay's old iron mining railway.

Walk 36

•DISTANCE•	7¾ miles (12.5km)
•MINIMUM TIME•	3hrs 45min
•ASCENT / GRADIENT•	820ft (250m) ▲▲ ▲
•LEVEL OF DIFFICULTY•	🚶 🚶 🚶
•PATHS•	Small but clear paths, some tracks, 1 stile
•LANDSCAPE•	Shingle beaches, woodland and moorland
•SUGGESTED MAP•	aqua3 OS Explorer 409 Raasay, Rona & Scalpay or 410 Skye – Portree & Bracadale
•START / FINISH•	Grid reference: NG 555342
•DOG FRIENDLINESS•	Close control in woodland and moor, on lead near livestock
•PARKING•	Ferry terminal at Sconser, Skye (or lay-by to east)
•PUBLIC TOILETS•	Sconser ferry terminal and start of walk

BACKGROUND TO THE WALK

In his *Journal of a Tour to the Hebrides with Dr Johnson* (1773), Scottish biographer James Boswell described the island of Raasay. 'It was a most pleasing approach to Raasay. We saw before us a beautiful bay, well defended with a rocky coast; a good gentleman's house, a fine verdure about it, a considerable number of trees, and beyond it hills and mountains in gradation of wildness. Our boatmen sung with great spirit.'

Boswell and Macleod

Boswell found Raasay a delight. He enjoyed the company of Macleod the laird and his ten beautiful daughters, he was impressed by the fine food and the two pet parrots, he enjoyed the landscape and he very much enjoyed his walk. He rose before six and, after a light breakfast of dry bread and whisky, set off with the laird. Boswell wore his usual walking gear of heavy coat, waistcoat and breeches, knee-boots, three-cornered hat and wig. The aim was the island's highest point, Dun Caan. Once there, they lunched on cold mutton and brandy, and danced a Highland reel on its flat summit. They returned by way of Beinn a' Chapuill, and in the afternoon 'there came a heavy rain, by which we were a great deal wet.' Their walk totalled 24 miles altogether (nearly 40km). By way of a warm-down, Boswell 'exerted himself extraordinarily in dancing, drinking porter heavily'.

'If I had my wife and little daughters with me, I would stay long enough,' said Boswell. And today Raasay, with its well-laid paths (22 of them, all together), its woodlands and moors and small beaches, offers walking for everyone, with none of the mainland's turgid bog and skin-shredding gabbro.

Boswell and his companion Dr Johnson felt highly honoured by the boatman who ferried them to Raasay, for just 27 years before, the sailor had carried the Bonnie Prince in the opposite direction. Prince Charles Stuart had sheltered on Raasay for as long as was safe, then crossed to the mainland and walked across the moors to Strath. The boatman told Boswell that the prince had been a stronger walker than himself, but that he'd had to dissuade him from littering the countryside with his empty brandy bottle. Even today, some walkers need similar education.

Raasay Reprisals

As punishment for sheltering the prince, the island was stripped of its cattle and every house burnt. The restoration of Raasay House was almost complete when Boswell visited. He had just one complaint. While the ruins of the former castle boasted an ancient garderobe, the new house had no such 'convenience', and Johnson reproached the laird accordingly. 'You take very good care of one end of a man, but not of the other!'

Walk 36 Directions

① CalMac ferries run roughly hourly during the day to the island of Raasay. Turn left on the island's small road. At **Inverarish**, turn left over a bridge and divert left along the shore. After a playing field you rejoin the road, which leads past the **Isle of Raasay Hotel** to another road junction.

Walk 36

② **Uamh na Ramh souterrain** is over a stile on the left. Continue ahead past the superb but neglected stable block, towards **Raasay House**, now an outdoor centre. Just before it, turn left to the old pier. A track continues below the ramparts of an old gun battery decorated with an iron mermaid. Follow a path around the bay, until a gate leads to a pleasant shoreline path to **Eilean Aird nan Gobhar**. Check the tides before crossing the rocks to this tidal island.

③ Head inland over a rock knoll, then pass along the left-hand edge of a plantation on a muddy path overhung by rhododendron. Continue along the shore of **North Bay**, with a pine plantation on your right, round to a headland. Go up briefly through the low basalt cliff and return along its top. Head along the left edge of the plantation, to emerge through a decorative iron gate on to a road.

④ Turn left for 180yds (165m) to a grey gate on the right. A green track leads up and to the right into a craggy valley. At a walled paddock it turns left to join a tarred road. Follow this down past a lily lochan and turn left across its dam. Join a wide path running up under larch and rhododendron but, in 100yds (91m), bear right, waymarked 'Temptation Hill Trail'. Look out for

WHAT TO LOOK FOR

Seals and **otters** play in North Bay. A seal will usually show only its dark brown head, often lifting it far out of the water because it's probably as interested in you as you are in it. An otter is less common, but if you do get a sighting it may be a good one as it plays among offshore boulders. Shoreline otters, with a ready escape out to sea, are less timid than ones in rivers.

a side path on the right which leads up to the remains of an Iron-Age broch (tower). The main path leads down to pass an austere white church, then bends to the right and drops to a tarred road.

⑤ Turn sharp left up the road for 200yds (183m), then right at a white-topped waymark. The track shrinks to a path as it bends left and climbs quite steeply. It becomes a forest track, passing more white waymarkers, finally reaching the abandoned buildings of an old iron mine.

WHERE TO EAT AND DRINK

Raasay House is now an outdoor centre and at its **Dolphin Café** you can enjoy fresh coffee where James Boswell and Dr Samuel Johnson danced with the ten beautiful Macleod daughters and dined on brandy, mutton chops, claret and punch.

WHILE YOU'RE THERE

'A little off the shore is a kind of subterraneous house. There has been a natural fissure or separation of the rock, running towards the sea, roofed over with long stones, and above them turf... in that place the inhabitants used to keep their oars.' Forgotten since Boswell's time, this **souterrain** has been rediscovered at Point ②.

⑥ At the tarred road beyond, turn up left to a signpost for the **Miners' Trail**. Here turn right on the green track of a former railway. Where a viaduct has been removed, the path scrambles down steeply and then climbs again to regain the railbed. The blue-waymarked Miners' Trail turns off, but your route follows the railway onwards, across a stretch of moor and down to the ferry terminal.

Seeing Sea Eagles at Portree Bay

A coastal walk to a raised beach called the Bile, then returning by way of Ben Chracaig.

•DISTANCE•	2¾ miles (4.4km)
•MINIMUM TIME•	1hr 15min
•ASCENT / GRADIENT•	400ft (122m) ▲▲▲
•LEVEL OF DIFFICULTY•	🚶 🚶 🚶
•PATHS•	Smooth, well-made paths, farm track, 3 stiles
•LANDSCAPE•	Views across Minch from wooded coast and hill above
•SUGGESTED MAP•	aqua3 OS Explorer 409 Raasay, Rona & Scalpay or 410 Skye – Portree & Bracadale
•START / FINISH•	Grid reference: NG 485436
•DOG FRIENDLINESS•	On leads through farmland, scoop poop on shore path
•PARKING•	Daytime-only parking on main A855 above Portree Harbour. Small parking area at slipway
•PUBLIC TOILETS•	Town centre

BACKGROUND TO THE WALK

While walking beside Portree Bay, keep at least one eye looking out to sea. You may spot what has been described as Britain's greatest conservation story – ever.

Sea Eagle Story

The last sea eagle in Scotland died on Skye in the early 1900s. Like all large raptors, it was shot at by shepherds and gamekeepers. An attempt to reintroduce them in 1959 was unsuccessful. In 1975, a secret RAF mission flew four young birds from Norway to the island of Rum. Over the next ten years, they were joined by 80 more. Today, about a dozen pairs are nesting, with a total population of around 100 spread up the western coast and the Hebrides.

In Gaelic it is called 'iolaire suil na greine' – the eagle with the sunlit eye – as its eye is a golden colour. In English it's also called the white-tailed eagle, the white-tailed fish eagle and the European sea eagle; it hasn't been back here long enough to finalise its name. Its nickname is the 'flying barn door' because it's so big, but it's not a heavy bird. Even with its 8ft (2.4m) wingspan, it weighs in at just 7lb (3kg). The sea eagle nests in cliffs. One nest, with an RSPB hide, is at Loch Frisa on Mull, another here at Portree. The Aros visitor centre has a closed-circuit TV camera trained on the nest, and the Portree fisherman have taken to throwing seafood to the birds outside the bay. The eagle feeds by snatching fish out of the sea – but even more spectacular is its mating display, when the two birds soar and cartwheel high above the water.

Was That An Eagle?

The first few eagles you think you see are almost certainly buzzards. When you see a real eagle, and even though you can't tell how far away it is, you'll know it for what it is. It's four times the size of a buzzard and its wingbeats are so slow and powerful. That's when it isn't gliding from one horizon to the other apparently without moving a feather. The sea eagle is even bigger than the golden one, and has a white tail – but so does a young golden eagle. But if the eagle is flying over the sea, and specially if it's over the sea at Portree, then it's a sea eagle.

Naturalists believed that the bird's main problem would be the golden eagle, which during the years of extinction has taken over the nest sites. But sadly, the real enemy is still humans. In 2000, and despite a 24-hour guard, thieves took the two eggs from the Mull pair.

Walk 37 Directions

① Turn off the main **A855** on a lane signed 'Budh Mor', down to the shoreline and continue to a small parking area. A tarred path continues along the shore. After a footbridge, it passes under hazels which show the ground-branching

habit of bushes formerly coppiced, cut back every seven years for firewood. The path then rounds the headland to reach the edge of a level green field called **the Bile**.

② A wall runs up the edge of the Bile. Ignore a small gate, but turn left with the wall on your right. Just before the field corner you pass a

Walk 37

large fuchsia bush, spectacular in mid-summer. About 25yds (23m) later the path forks. Turn right, crossing a small stream and the wall, to head along the top edge of the Bile. Turn right, down a fence, to a field gate. Cross the top of the next field on an old green path, to a stile at its corner. You will see a track just beyond.

> **WHERE TO EAT AND DRINK** ℹ
> The informal Well Plaid bar/restaurant is at the **Royal Hotel** above the harbour. On the pier itself is the **Lower Deck** seafood restaurant, with a chip shop for those in a hurry. Near the start of the walk is the **Cuillin Hills Hotel**, a former MacDonald hunting lodge, now serving good bar meals.

③ Turn sharp left, up the track. At the top it passes through two gates to reach a stony road just to right of **Torvaig**. Turn left past the house and cross the foot of a tarred road into a gently descending track. It runs down between two large corrugated sheds and through to a gate with a stile.

④ The grassy path ahead leads down into Portree, but you can take a short, rather rough, diversion to **Dun Torvaig** (an ancient fortified hilltop) above. For the dun, turn left along the fence, and left again on a well-made path above. It leads to a kissing gate above the two sheds. Turn sharp right along the fence for

a few steps, then bear left around the base of a small outcrop and head straight up on a tiny path to the dun. Remnants of dry-stone walling can be seen around the summit. Return to the gravel path, passing above Point ④ to join the wall on the right. The path leads down under goat willows into a wood where it splits; stay close to the wall.

⑤ At the first houses (**The Parks Bungalow 5**), keep downhill on a tarred street. On the left is the entrance to the **Cuillin Hills Hotel**. A few steps later, fork right on to a stony path. At the shore road, turn right across a stream and at once right again on a path that runs up for 60yds (55m) to a craggy little waterfall. Return to the shore road and turn right to the walk start.

> **WHAT TO LOOK FOR** ℹ
> The strangely level meadow called the Bile is a **raised beach** that formed during the ice age. As the ice melted, the sea level rose, but at the same time, the land rose much further as the weight of overlying ice was removed. The result is that this former beach is now 100ft (30m) above the sea.

> **WHILE YOU'RE THERE** ℹ
> The **Aros Experience**, just south of Portree, has the RSPB's closed circuit TV link with the sea-eagle nest. Nest action is between April and July (the young hatch in April). The centre also has an exhibition and audio-visual centre dedicated to the people of Skye, including Bonnie Prince Charlie. Outside there are some short forest walks.

Waterstein Head

Through crofting country and peat moors to a 1,000ft (305m) sea cliff.

•DISTANCE•	5¾ miles (9.2km)
•MINIMUM TIME•	3hrs 30min
•ASCENT / GRADIENT•	1,500ft (457m) ▲▲▲
•LEVEL OF DIFFICULTY•	🚶🚶
•PATHS•	Grassy clifftops and moorland, 1 stile
•LANDSCAPE•	Clifftops high above Atlantic Ocean
•SUGGESTED MAP•	aqua3 OS Explorer 407 Skye – Dunvegan
•START / FINISH•	Grid reference: NG 163443
•DOG FRIENDLINESS•	Mostly on lead – risk of scaring sheep over cliff edges
•PARKING•	Ramasaig road end or pull-ins at pass ¾ mile (1.2km) north
•PUBLIC TOILETS•	None on route

BACKGROUND TO THE WALK

After the defeat of Bonnie Prince Charlie's uprising in 1746, the clan system was swept away. But the clansmen were still there, transformed into crofters. Elsewhere, such subsistence smallholders go by the honourable name of 'peasant farmers', with 25 acres (10ha), a kailyard, a cow and some sheep on the hill.

The Crofters

Rents rose, partly to support the landlords' new London lifestyles. Crofting lands were cleared to make way for sheep, and the crofters were forced to relocate, first to the shore and later right out of the country to Canada and Australia. By the late 1800s, they were starting to fight back. In 1882, crofters at the Braes, south of Portree, resisted an eviction. Fifty Glasgow policemen were sent to restore order, and in the 'Battle of the Braes' the crofters retaliated with sticks and stones.

In Glendale, land-starved crofters deliberately let their cattle stray on to neighbouring farms. Government forces and the gunboat *Jackal* were defied by 600 crofters. There were four arrests, including John Macpherson, the 'Glendale Martyr', and a minister, the Reverend D MacCallum. The 'martyrs' received two-month prison sentences. The public outcry that followed saw a newly formed 'Crofters' Party' – distant forerunner of today's New Labour – send four MPs to Westminster. The first of the Crofting Acts, passed by Gladstone's government, led to less unfair rents and security of tenure.

Today, thanks to those battles of long ago, Glendale and the Braes are inhabited lands where so much of Scotland is bleak and empty. Crofters now have the right to buy and enjoy subsidies and grants from the government. Few crofts provide enough to live on, without a part-time job on the side. As a result there's a series of small-scale, off-beat and interesting tourist enterprises along the Glendale Trail.

Peat became the crofters' fuel supply and in a few places it is still being worked today, often where a modern road runs beside one of the remaining peat banks. Above Loch Eishort on this walk you'll see the little triangular stacks, each made from four peats, drying in the wind (and of course getting wet again in the rain). And when it burns, it brings the smell of the wild bog-moss right into the house.

TRIG POINT
296
④

WATERSTEIN HEAD

BEINN CHARNACH

⑤

250

Dunvegan, Glendale

▲ 278
Beinn nan Corrafidheag

Moonen Bay

BEINN NA COINNICH

LOCH EISHORT

MOONEN BURN

▲ 311
Ben Vratabreck

P

③

P

RAMASAIG CLIFF

Ramasaig

①

Ⓐ

RAMASAIG BURN

▲ 170

②

Ramasaig Bay

WATERFALLS

HOE RAPE

Ⓔ

Ⓑ

The Hoe
▲ 231

Ⓓ

Ⓒ

LORGILL VALLEY

LORGILL BAY

-N-

0   ½ Mile

0   1 Km

Walk 38 **Directions**

① From the end of the tarmac, the road continues as a track between farm buildings, with a bridge over the **Ramasaig Burn**. After a gate it reaches a shed with a tin roof. Bear right here and follow the left bank of Ramasaig Burn to the shore.

WHERE TO EAT AND DRINK ⓘ

An Strupag Gallery and café at Glendale sells home-made cakes. Dunvegan's hotels all serve food. The **Misty Isle Hotel** is inexpensive and **Dunvegan Hotel**'s restaurant has a sea view and special menu section for those 'who do not care for seafood or haggis'.

---

② Cross the burn at a ford and head up a very steep meadow beside the fence that protects the cliff edge. There's an awkward fence to cross half way up. At the top, above **Ramasaig Cliff**, keep following the fence on the left. It cuts across to the right to protect a notch in the cliff edge. From here (Point ③), you could cut down to the parking areas at the road pass near by.

③ Keep downhill along the cliffside fence. At the bottom, a turf wall off to the right provides another short-cut back to the road. The clifftop walk now bears slightly right around the V-notch of the **Moonen Burn**. A small path crosses the stream and continues uphill to

---

WHAT TO LOOK FOR ⓘ

Between the cliffs and the road is soggy peat, but the well-drained cliff edge grows short-cropped grass, along with tiny **meadow flowers**, such as pale pink thyme and tiny white eyebright. Five-petalled yellow tormentil, a member of the rose family, also grows here, and is common on the open moor.

---

rejoin the clifftop fence, which soon turns slightly inland around another cliff notch. The cliff-edge fence leads up and to the left, to reach **Waterstein Head**. Here there is a trig point, 971ft (296m) above the sea – the second highest sea cliff on Skye. Below you will see Neist Point lighthouse.

④ Return for ¼ mile (400m) down to where the fence bends to the right, then continue ahead through a shallow grassy col for the slight rise to **Beinn Charnach**. Here bear right to follow a gently rounded grass ridge line parallel with the cliffs. The highest line along the ridge is the driest. A fence runs across, with a grey gate at its highest point where it passes through a col. Climb over the gate and on up to a cairn on **Beinn na Coinnich**.

WHILE YOU'RE THERE ⓘ

Dunvegan Castle is one of Scotland's most visited attractions. For those who prefer the quirky and out-of-the-way, the Glendale Visitor Route includes the small **Colbost Folk Museum** and the centre devoted to the famous MacCrimmons of Borreraig, hereditary clan of pipers. The **Giant MacAskill Museum**, Dunvegan, in a re-antiquated black house, is a small museum to a big man, whose height of 7ft 9in (239cm) got him into the *Guinness Book of Records*.

---

⑤ Continue along the slightly rocky plateau for 300yds (274m) to the south east top. Now the Ramasaig road is visible ¼ mile (400m) away on the left. Go down to join a quad bike track heading towards the road. Just before reaching the road, the bike track crosses a swampy col. This shows old and recent peat workings. Turn right, along the road, passing above **Loch Eishort** to the start.

High Cliffs at Hoe Rape

An abandoned valley leads to black sea cliffs above the Atlantic.
See map and information panel for Walk 38

•DISTANCE•	5¼ miles (8.4km)
•MINIMUM TIME•	3hrs 15min
•ASCENT / GRADIENT•	902ft (275m) ▲▲▲
•LEVEL OF DIFFICULTY•	🚶 🚶 🚶

Walk 39 Directions
(Walk 38 option)

From the road end (Point ①), head down the track between farm buildings and across **Ramasaig Burn** to a stone shed with a tin roof – a former black house (Point Ⓐ). This is where Walk 38 turns right, but continue slightly left on the main track. At the next right-hand bend of the track, the hummocks of former lazybed cultivation are above on the left. The track crosses a ford and climbs over moorland, descending to a gate (Point Ⓑ), with a view into Lorgill Valley.

Don't go through the gate but turn right on a trace of path. The way now follows the top of the steep ground, with the **Lorgill Valley** below on the left. This former settlement has just one building remaining, another former black house, re-roofed in slate. Old field enclosures and lazybeds can be clearly seen. Behind, the moor rises in terraces and long, low outcrops – typical lava landscape (► Walk 33).

Follow the top edge of one such outcrop, then a grassed-over old wall. Where this wall line appears to vanish, go up a few steps to find it again above a trickle waterfall. The wall line crosses an incised stream. At a second stream, the wall heads off to the right, away from the drop to Lorgill. Keep ahead, climbing a little, sticking to the valley rim. Follow the top of a line of outcrops round the point above **Lorgill Bay** (Point Ⓒ). Look back along the coast to see the tall sea-stacks called Macleod's Maidens, visible from this one point on the walk.

The way is now clear, keeping to the short grass near the edge of tremendous cliffs on the left. The ground rises gently to an old wall (Point Ⓓ), then starts to drop. A fence running across guards a large notch in the cliff edge, so keep round to its right. With the cliffs now much lower, you can head out left on to the grassy promontory of **Hoe Rape** (Point Ⓔ).

Continue along the shoreline, around **Ramasaig Bay**, crossing more lazybed hummocks. Cross a stream to a field gate and turn left along the fence to the **Ramasaig Burn** (Point ②). The stream plunges to the beach in a waterfall, which was seen from Hoe Rape, but isn't visible from above. Don't cross, but turn up alongside the stream to the farm buildings at **Ramasaig** – or continue with Walk 38.

Walk 40

Loch Shieldaig's Shores

A walk around the many inlets of the Shieldaig peninsula.

•DISTANCE•	3¼ miles (5.3km)
•MINIMUM TIME•	1hr 45min
•ASCENT / GRADIENT•	500ft (152m) ▲ ▲ ▲
•LEVEL OF DIFFICULTY•	🚶 🚶 🚶
•PATHS•	Well-made old paths, one rough section, no stiles
•LANDSCAPE•	Saltwater views up Loch Torridon and down Loch Shieldaig
•SUGGESTED MAP•	aqua3 OS Explorer 428 Kyle of Lochalsh
•START / FINISH•	Grid reference: NG 814538
•DOG FRIENDLINESS•	On leads in village and when passing livestock
•PARKING•	South end of Shieldaig village, opposite shop and hotel
•PUBLIC TOILETS•	North end of village (another car park)

Walk 40 Directions

A hundred years ago, all you needed to connect your cottage to civilisation was a well-made path to keep your feet dry. Today, a powerboat to the nearby pier is the preferred way to visit the neighbours and bring home the shopping. However, the paths to two cottages north of Shieldaig village are still there to be walked: a single path at first, that divides at the base of the Shieldaig promontory to form a Y-shape. No historic path links the two top points of the Y, so for this short section of the walk the going is rather rougher.

WHAT TO LOOK FOR ⓘ

Look and listen for **eider ducks** and **divers**. The male eider is black-and-white, the female an inconspicuous brown and their call is a sort of *coo-ing* murmur. On a still evening, a flock of eider out on the loch is the softest sound ever. If you hear a wild, haunting cry that could be a lamenting mermaid, it's probably a black-throated diver.

Place names ending in 'aig' (the equivalent of the Norse 'vik') are Norse harbours. So Shieldaig (Shill Vik) is Herring Harbour. Follow the village street along the shoreline. At the village end it rises slightly, with another parking area, and a war memorial above on the right.

The village school is ahead; just before it, turn right up a rough track. The track passes a couple of houses to turn left. In another 100yds (91m) it divides and here the main track for Rubha Lodge forks off left, but your route bears right, passing to the right of a glacier-smoothed rock knoll.

Offshore, densely wooded Shieldaig island shows how rich the natural vegetation would be without grazing deer and sheep. All over the Highlands, projects to fence off some of the lower hill slopes are aiming to re-create tree-clad scenes of 2,000 years ago. It isn't even necessary to replant as pockets of remaining forest and trees on crags away from the nibblers spread seed naturally into the protected areas.

The terraced path runs through birch woods, near the top of the shore slope with the sea just below. It emerges to cross a level grassy area, then goes slightly uphill through a gap between pinkish rocks, to pass above the head of another bay. The way then strikes across a peat bog. In the middle of this flat area it divides at a cairn. (The branch on the left will be the return route.)

WHILE YOU'RE THERE ⓘ

The natural tree cover of the Highlands is pine, oak or birch, depending on the local climate. Ancient **ashwood** is a surprise. Rassal ashwood grows on a small outcrop of limestone and pollen in peat sediments suggests it's 6,000 years old. Now fenced as a National Nature Reserve, it is regrowing its original limestone-loving wild flowers. The reserve's small car park is on the single-track A896 (grid ref NG 840432).

The right-hand path runs along the left edge of the peaty area, with rocky ground above on its left. Ahead on the right are the grass hummocks of former cultivation (lazybeds) running down to a bay on the north side of the promontory. Now the pink-surfaced path runs next to birch trees for 50yds (46m). Look out carefully for the point where it becomes peaty with a rock formation like a low ruin on its right as here is an easily missed path junction. What seems like the main path, ahead and slightly downhill, peters out eventually. The correct path forks off to the left, slanting up to the higher ground just above.

The path is now clear, crossing slabby ground in the direction of the peninsula's **trig point**, ¼ mile (400m) away. Shortly it rises a little

to a gateway in a former fence. Here it curves to the right, down through an outcrop, then bends left. Aiming to the right of the still-conspicuous trig point, it crosses a small heather moor and a boggy area. At a broken wall, the path turns down right through a gap to the top of a grassy meadow. The first of two shoreline cottages, **Bad-callda**, is just below.

Rough paths lead to the left across the boggy top of the meadow and then pass above a birchwood, with the trig point just above on the left. A branch path lets you scramble up to the trig point over heather and glacier-smoothed rocks. The main route, however, keeps forward at the same level to a heather knoll with a pole on it. Just below is a second cottage, **Camas-ruadh**, with its green bay and tidal islet.

The path zig-zags down between rocks to pass to the right of the cottage. White paint spots lead to the right of a shed to a wall gap. Turn left, behind the shed, to join a path coming from the cottage.

The return path is easy to follow, with the cottage's phone line always near by on the left. Cross two peaty moors, then go up a rocky mound just to the right of the telephone poles. The path passes through shoreline birches, then runs above them. It bends left over a slight rise, then drops quite steeply to rejoin the outward route at the cairn.

WHERE TO EAT AND DRINK ⓘ

The restaurant and Shieldaig Bar at **Tigh an Eilean Hotel** in Shieldaig serve home-cooked food using produce from the sea, river and hill. You can also get tea, coffee – and more seafood – at **Shieldaig Salmon**, on the main road outside the village (summer only).

Walk 41

Coire Lair and the Coulin Forest

Deer stalkers' paths lead into the heart of the South Torridon mountains.

•DISTANCE•	9 miles (14.5km)
•MINIMUM TIME•	5hrs
•ASCENT / GRADIENT•	1,700ft (518m) ▲▲▲
•LEVEL OF DIFFICULTY•	🚶🚶 🚶🚶 🚶🚶
•PATHS•	Well-made path, then track, no stiles
•LANDSCAPE•	Boulder-scattered moorland between high hills
•SUGGESTED MAP•	aqua3 OS Explorer 429 Glen Carron & West Monar
•START / FINISH•	Grid reference: NH 005484
•DOG FRIENDLINESS•	Under control in deer forest
•PARKING•	On A890 below Achnashellach Station
•PUBLIC TOILETS•	None on route
•NOTE•	During stalking season on Achnashellach Estate (15 September–20 October, not Sundays), keep strictly to route, which is right of way.

BACKGROUND TO THE WALK

The path winds up from Strath Carron into Coire Lair. The corrie is a fine one, with scattered pines, waterfalls and craggy mountains. The path that takes you there is also good – as well-built and thoughtfully routed as any resurfaced path of today. It's terraced at the steep places, drained at the level places and avoids the boggy places altogether. Over a century old, it was built not for walkers but stalkers – or rather for their sturdy Highland ponies bringing down a deer corpse weighing 2cwt (100kg) or more.

Deer stalking calls on the legs and the intelligence in equal measure, appealing to man's ancient hunting urges. 'The beautiful motions of the deer, his sagacity and the skilful generalship that can alone ensure success in the pursuit of him, keep the mind in a pleasurable state of constant excitement'. Thus said William Scrope Esq, in the book *Days of Deerstalking*, which presented this sport to the leisured and affluent of 1845.

Red Bedrock

As the path rises above the tree line, you'll notice slabs of Torridonian sandstone underfoot – the ghillies have deliberately routed it over this maintenance-free surface. On the left, Fuar Tholl (the name means 'cold hole') is of the same red rock, but ahead on the right, Beinn Liath Mhor is composed of pale Cambrian quartzite. As you top the pass and look east, the hills ahead are rounded, grey and slightly less exciting all the way to the North Sea.

As you come to know Scotland you realise that all the way along its north-western edge there's a zone of rather special hills. Applecross, Torridon, the Great Wilderness, Coigach, Inverpolly: these names mean sandstone and quartzite to the geologist, and pure magic to the mountaineer.

The rest of the Northern Highlands is made of a speckly grey rock – Moinian schist. The boundary line is the Moine Thrust. It's called a 'thrust' because these grey mountains have been pushed in over the top of the Torridonian red and the Cambrian white. It marks the western limit of the crumple zone from when England crashed into Scotland 400 million years ago. On the face of Beinn Liath Mhor, the arrival of the Moinian has crumpled the quartzite, like a boot landing on a carelessly placed cheese sandwich. A short wander from Point ③ further into the corrie will show this more clearly, and you'll also see the famous Mainreachan Buttress on the north side of Fuar Tholl.

Walk 41 Directions

① The track to the station runs up behind a red phone box, then turns right to reach the platform end.

Cross the line through two gates and head up the stony track opposite, past a waymarker arrow. After 100yds (91m) you reach a junction under low-voltage power lines. Turn left here on a smooth gravel road to a gate through a deer fence. After ¼ mile (400m), look out for a cairn where a new path turns back to the left.

② This path goes back through the deer fence at a kissing gate, then runs up alongside the **River Lair**. As the slope steepens above the tree-line, a short side path on the left gives a view of a waterfall. The well-maintained stalkers' path runs over slabs of bare sandstone. A cairn marks the point where it arrives in the upper valley, **Coire Lair**, with a view to the high pass at its head, 2 miles (3.2km) away.

WHERE TO EAT AND DRINK ⓘ
The **Strathcarron Hotel** at Strathcarron Station serves home cooking and real ales in its restaurant, bar (dogs and children welcome) and coffee shop. **Loch Carron Hotel** at Lochcarron village does good bar meals and also welcomes children and dogs.

③ About 200yds (183m) after this first cairn, another marks a junction of paths. Bear right here, between two pools. Shortly there is a second junction with a cairn. Bear right, on a path that leaves the corrie through a wide, shallow col just 350yds (320m) above. An elegant conical cairn marks the highest point. The path runs downhill among drumlins and sandstone boulders, slanting down to the right to join the wooded **Allt na Dearcag**. The path now runs down alongside this stream; you may notice pale grey quartzite underfoot here. A scattered forest damaged by fire and by grazing deer is on the opposite side as the path drops to reach a footbridge. This bridge crosses a side stream, the **Allt Coire Beinne Leithe**, with the **Easan Geal**, White Waterfalls, just above.

WHILE YOU'RE THERE ⓘ
Strome Castle stands on a romantic headland overlooking the narrows of Loch Carron. It was besieged by the Mackenzies in 1602, and surrendered after some 'silly women' poured drinking water into the gunpowder. The Mackenzies blew it up, but left enough of the walls to make a fine foreground for views along the loch.

④ At a locked estate hut, a track continues downhill, with the gorge of the **Easan Dorcha** (Dark Waterfalls) on its right. After a mile (1.6km) there's a stone bridge on the right. Turn across this, on to a track that runs up the wide, open valley to the **Coulin Pass** at its head. Coulin, pronounced Cowlinn, is the name of the deer forest, the river and the loch at its foot. Gaelic 'Cuilion' means holly tree.

⑤ After the pass, the track goes through a gate into plantations, then bends right to slant down the side of Strath Carron. At a Scottish Rights of Way Society signpost, follow the main track ahead towards **Achnashellach**. A clear-felled area gives views to the left, just before you cross a bridge to reach a mobile phone mast. Fork left, passing a second mast, and descend gently to reach the junction above **Achnashellach Station**.

WHAT TO LOOK FOR ⓘ
The hill on the left as you enter Coire Lair is **Fuar Tholl**. A rocky projection seen from Glen Carron is known as **Wellington's Nose**, in commemoration of the duke who defeated Napoleon in 1815. From Coire Lair, it reveals itself as the top of the steep Mainreachan Buttress. The first climbers to venture there in the 1960s found classic routes of middling difficulty. Today, it's climbed even when covered in winter ice.

Following the Diabaig Coast Path

A walk above Loch Torridon in the footsteps of the fairy folk – the legendary duine sithe.

•DISTANCE•	9½ miles (15.3km)
•MINIMUM TIME•	6hrs
•ASCENT / GRADIENT•	1,805ft (550m) ▲▲▲
•LEVEL OF DIFFICULTY•	🏃 🏃 🏃
•PATHS•	Narrow, rough and wet in places, no stiles
•LANDSCAPE•	Rocky knolls and small lochans
•SUGGESTED MAP•	aqua3 OS Explorer 433 Torridon – Beinn Eighe & Liathach
•START / FINISH•	Grid reference: NG 840575
•DOG FRIENDLINESS•	On lead passing Alligin Shuas; close control near sheep
•PARKING•	Informal camp and caravan site above Inveralligin
•PUBLIC TOILETS•	None on route or near by

BACKGROUND TO THE WALK

New Year's Eve in Wester Ross is a time when old songs are sung, whisky is drunk (not all of it approved by the exciseman either) and tales are told in both English and Gaelic. Over the years these stories mature and grow, and also change location, so that the tailor who lost his hump to the fairies lived not only in Scotland, but in Ireland and even Italy. Today it is categorised as 'folktale type 503'.

Fairy Tales and Ghosts

Many of the tales told in Alligin take place in the knolly, obviously magical ground on the way to Diabaig. One story concerns two men of the village who were bringing whisky for the New Year from Gairloch by way of the coast path. They heard wonderful music and came upon a cave in the hill where the fairy people had started their Hogmanay celebrations a few hours early. Fascinated, the man with the keg crept closer and closer until he was actually inside, whereupon the cave closed up and disappeared. A year later the other man came back, found the cave open again and managed to drag his friend out across the threshold. The friend thought he'd been in there only a few minutes, but of the whisky he carried there was no trace.

At the top of the hill road is tiny Lochan Dearg, and here there is a ghost that appears only to people bearing his own name, Murdo Mackenzie. The kilted spirit, one of the Mackenzies of Gairloch, was slain by a Torridon MacDonald and buried somewhere near by.

Horse Tale

Loch Diabaigas Airde (Point ③) is haunted by the water spirit called the kelpie. This appears as a magnificent white horse, but if you mount it, the horse gallops rapidly into the loch and you're never seen again. That is, unless you just happen to have a bridle that's made of pure silver to tame it. Another kelpie lives in the Lochan Toll nam Beiste, the Lochan of the Beast Hole, at the back of Beinn Alligin.

How to Protect Yourself from the Duine Sithe

Be polite, but don't accept food from them. At best it'll be cow dung, at worst it'll enslave you for ever. Carry iron, oatmeal or a groundsel root for protection, and a cry of 'am monadh oirbh, a' bheistein' ('back to the hill, you wee beastie') is effective. Approaching Alligin Shuas, walk carefully past Cnoc nan Sithe, the Fairy Knoll. Fairy music has been heard above the gorge of the Alligin burn.

Walk 42 **Directions**

① Follow the road right, past the village green and over the **Abhainn Alligin**. A path leads along the shoreline for 100yds (91m), then makes its way up right among sandstone outcrops. Bear left under a power line to join the corner of a tarmac driveway. Keep ahead to **Alligin Shuas**.

Walk 42

② Turn up the road and then left, on the road for **Diabaig**. As the road steepens, you can take a path ahead, rejoining the road as it crosses a high pass and runs down past two lochs – Loch Diabaigas Airde and Loch a'Mhullaich – which are linked.

③ Turn off left, crossing the outflow of **Loch a'Mhullaich** on a footbridge. A clear path leads out along the high wall of a stream valley, then zig-zags down a spur, aiming for a grey gate. Go down through woods to a white house, **No 1 Diabaig**. Turn right to reach the old stone pier.

WHILE YOU'RE THERE ℹ
The National Trust for Scotland has a **countryside centre** at Torridon village, right below the frowning sandstone wall of Liathach (open May–September). It has audio-visual displays on the scenery and wildlife, with an unstaffed deer museum close by.

---

④ Return up the path you just came down to pass a stone shed. Here a sign indicates a turn to the right, under an outcrop and between boulders. The path heads up to a small rock step with an arrow mark and a convenient tree root which you can use to hold on to. It then leads up to a gate in a fence and zig-zags into an open gully with a large crag on the right.

WHAT TO LOOK FOR ℹ
The walk passes through grey **Lewisian gneiss**, worn into its present knolly shapes by glaciers. But is it grey? Look closely and you will see it has zig-zag stripes of many colours, like tweed. This is the oldest rock in Britain and it is made of other, even older, rocks that have been bashed about through half the history of the planet.

At the top of this, it turns right along a shelf, with still more crag above. The path slants gently down along the foot of another crag, then up to a col.

⑤ From here the path is small but clear. It bends right to **Loch a' Bhealaich Mhoir** and then turns left below it to reach yet another small loch. Follow its stream down towards the cottage of **Port Lair**.

⑥ Pass above the house, then slant gradually up away from the sea. The path crosses the head of a bracken valley with a ruined croft house into a bleak knolly area out of sight of the sea. Cross two branches of a stream and go up to a cairn which marks where the path bears left up the spur. It now contours across a heathery meadow among the knolls, at the end of which it climbs pink rocks over a final spur. Here there is a good view up Loch Torridon to Liathach for the first time.

WHERE TO EAT AND DRINK ℹ
Mrs Ross at **Ben Bhraggie** in Diabaig sometimes offers teas. Look for the notice outside the house. But carry a picnic in case, as the next shop is at Torridon village.

---

⑦ The path descends slightly to cross a high, steep slope of heather. Near the end of this slope, the path forks. Take the upper branch, to go through a wide col. The rather boggy path heads down towards **Alligin Shuas**. From a gate above the village, a faint path runs down in the direction of a distant green shed. It descends through a wood, then contours just above the village to reach the road above Point ②. Retrace your steps to the start of the walk.

Flowerdale Falls

Porpoise-watching along the Gairloch shore, then up a rocky valley.

•DISTANCE•	5¼ miles (8.4km)
•MINIMUM TIME•	2hrs 45min
•ASCENT / GRADIENT•	800ft (244m) ▲ ▲ ▲
•LEVEL OF DIFFICULTY•	🚶🚶 🚶🚶 🚶🚶
•PATHS•	Tracks and smooth paths, mostly waymarked, no stiles
•LANDSCAPE•	Gentle river valley and rocky coast
•SUGGESTED MAP•	aqua3 OS Explorer 433 Torridon – Beinn Eighe & Liathach or 434 Gairloch & Loch Ewe
•START / FINISH•	Grid reference: NG 807756
•DOG FRIENDLINESS•	On lead past Flowerdale House (as signs indicate)
•PARKING•	Beach car park, southern end of Gairloch
•PUBLIC TOILETS•	Walk start and Charlestown pier

BACKGROUND TO THE WALK

On a calm day in 1809, three fisherman drowned in Loch Ewe when their small boat was attacked and sunk by a whale. These Hebridean waters are among the best in Europe for cetaceans (whales, dolphins and porpoises). The Gulf Stream brings warm, plankton-rich water and the swirling currents around the islands bring nutrients to the surface. The plankton flourish; the fish eat the plankton; the whales and dolphins eat the fish.

Porpoise or Dolphin?

The strongest currents are at headlands and narrow sea passages, so these are good places to look for marine wildlife. Calm days are best, and early morning best of all when looking west, as the low sunlight shines off their wet backs. On most summer days, either the harbour porpoise or common dolphin – or possibly both – can be seen, given a little patience, in Loch Gairloch.

But which is which? At 6ft (2m) or less, the porpoise is smaller. It has a short, stubby fin compared with the dolphin's more elegant one. Harbour porpoises are normally shy, but the ones at Gairloch are untypically friendly, often approaching boats. Endangered in the world as a whole, the ones at Gairloch are doing well and a Special Area of Conservation has been proposed for them here.

What the Future Holds

The whaling industry in Scotland ended in 1951, but serious threats remain. Dolphins and porpoises are accidentally caught in fishing nets and floating plastic rope and old nets are another danger. Pollution from agriculture and forestry releases heavy metals and pesticides into the ocean. Fish farming is also probably damaging the dolphins. More fish sewage than human sewage goes into the Hebridean seas, all of it untreated, and anti-fouling paint on fish farms contributes more chemical pollutants, pesticides and antibiotics.

Cetaceans use sound signals through the water for finding fish, as well as for communication. Human noise interference comes from ships, dredging nets, seismic oil exploration and seal scammers – underwater beepers fitted to fish farms.

We don't know how well the dolphins and porpoises are doing. The growth of the whale-spotting industry means that we are just starting to discover how the populations are growing or declining. Marine tourism is now a £9 million concern with 400 jobs. By going on one of these trips, you will probably become a dolphin enthusiast, but also contribute to crucial research. A responsible boatman will not pursue the animals or steer into the middle of a group, but move quietly and wait for the dolphins to approach the boat.

Walk 43

Walk 43 Directions

① Cross the road and head up to the right of the **cemetery**. Turn left at its corner, going into trees to a track above. Turn right until a footbridge leads on to a wide path that runs downhill. With a wall corner ahead, turn right (signed 'Flowerdale Waterfall'). A track runs down to a tarred driveway.

② Turn left to pass **Flowerdale House**. The way is marked with red-topped poles. The track passes to the left of a lovely old barn and turns right at another sign for the waterfall to pass **Flowerdale Mains**. In about ¼ mile (400m) you pass a concrete bridge on the right.

③ Follow the main path ahead, still to the left of the stream to reach a footbridge built by the Royal Engineers, just before you get to **Flowerdale Waterfall**.

WHAT TO LOOK FOR ⓘ

The **buzzard** often soars above the glen on wide, rounded wings and fanned tail. Like the much smaller kestrel, it can hover on fluttering wings while examining the ground below. In spring you may hear its mewing cry, not unlike a kitten. Once you're familiar with the buzzard, you'll have no trouble identifying the **golden eagle**, which looks similar but is three or four times the size.

---

④ The path leads up past the waterfall to cross a footbridge just above. It runs up into a pine clump, then turns back down the valley. After another footbridge it joins a rough track, which itself meets a forest road beside Point ③. Turn left, away from the concrete bridge, through felled forest that's being allowed to regenerate naturally with at least five separate species (birch, alder, pine, willow and rowan).

WHILE YOU'RE THERE ⓘ

The **Gairloch Marine Life Centre** has a display on cetaceans, seals and seabirds. It runs two-hour cruises on the *Starquest*, where you'll almost certainly see porpoises and seals, and possibly dolphins and minke whales. Every trip contributes to scientific knowledge of the wildlife populations. Cruises depend on the weather and are often fully booked.

---

⑤ Look out for a blue-topped pole marking a path on the right with a footbridge. It leads on through meadowland and bracken with blue waymarker poles. The path bends right at an old fence cornerpost and goes down through encroaching bracken and birch to pass above and to the left of an enclosed field. Turn right under two large oak trees and cross a small stream to an earth track.

⑥ Turn left for a few steps, until a small bracken path runs up to the right past a waymarked power pole. The path bends left under oaks, then drops to rejoin the earth track. This soon meets a larger track, which is the old road from Loch Maree to Gairloch. Turn right along this, through a couple of gates, to reach the **Old Inn** at Charlestown.

WHERE TO EAT AND DRINK ⓘ

The **Old Inn**, beside the former bridge over the Abhainn Ghlas in Charlestown, offers live music, fresh local seafood (including a cook-what-you-catch service), a barbecue grill and outdoor tables. Dogs are allowed in the outdoor section. The one thing it lacks, due to intervening buildings, is a sea view. **Flowerdale Mains farm** serves teas and snacks in summer.

---

⑦ Cross the old bridge, and the main road, to the pier. Turn right at a sign for Gairloch Chandlery, to find a tarmac path signposted for the beach. This passes to the left of a pinewood, then turns right into the trees. It bends left and emerges to run along the spine of a small headland. Just before being carried out to sea it turns sharp right, and crosses above a rocky bay to the fort (**An Dun**). A duckboard path runs along the back of the beach, then turns right to the car park.

A Gneiss Little Hill

A tough ascent past a waterfall on to a wild and rocky mountain.
See map and information panel for Walk 43

•DISTANCE•	7¼ miles (11.7km)
•MINIMUM TIME•	4hrs 30min
•ASCENT / GRADIENT•	1,800ft (548m) ▲▲▲
•LEVEL OF DIFFICULTY•	🚶🚶 🚶🚶 🚶🚶

Walk 44 Directions (Walk 43 option)

The Lewisian gneiss forms a particularly worn and wild landscape, all bare rock, bog and little pools. **An Groban** is a hill that's as rugged and romantic as a full mountain. This side-trip to reach it starts at Point ④, just before the Royal Engineers' footbridge. Turn left up the side stream on a small path. After a few steps it bears up left into woods above the stream – this part is steep, narrow and slippery. It regains the riverbank above the **Eas Dubh** (Black Waterfall). Keep on up to the left of the stream, to a deer fence (Point Ⓐ).

Fenced areas are great for regenerating birch and pine, but can be a nuisance for walkers. Flowerdale Estate has not only provided a ladder stile on this informal path, but also put very basic stiles all along their fencing – you can see one just across the stream. Above the stile, head up to the left of the braided rapids of the upper waterfall. Old metal fence posts show the way over rough ground to the left of a small pool with lilies. Cross the stream

(Point Ⓑ) before a larger lochan, and eye up the rocky cone of **An Groban** ahead.

The ascent is a set of zig-zags on grassy shelves. Head into a grassy valley that slants up to the right, just below the main rocky pyramid. Follow this to the small col at its top. From here you can look across the small **Gleann a'Ghrobain** to a similar small rocky mountain opposite, **Sidhean Mor**.

Turn up left, into an open grassy gully with a large cairn in its foot. Go up for 100yds (91m) to a red sandstone boulder in the middle of the little valley. Just above this, small cairns mark a path up to the right. This leads up to a small col, with a perched sandstone boulder on the left. Here the tiny path turns right for the last 90yds (82m) to the summit (Point Ⓒ), which has a stone trig point.

Look back and note the perched sandstone boulder. This is the important landmark for the return. Going back, you'll use the same route. Descend to the perched boulder and turn down left just before it. Small cairns and traces of path lead down to the head of the grassy gully, where you turn down left to the cairn at its foot.

Walk 45

Beinn Eighe Mountain Trail

The toughest waymarked trail in Scotland to a lunar landscape.

•DISTANCE•	3½ miles (5.7km)
•MINIMUM TIME•	2hrs 45min
•ASCENT / GRADIENT•	1,847ft (563m) ▲▲▲
•LEVEL OF DIFFICULTY•	👣👣 👣👣 👣
•PATHS•	Steep well-made path, no stiles
•LANDSCAPE•	Pine forest below, bare rock and stones above
•SUGGESTED MAP•	aqua3 OS Explorer 433 Torridon – Beinn Eighe & Liathach
•START / FINISH•	Grid reference: NH 002650
•DOG FRIENDLINESS•	Permitted only if under close control
•PARKING•	Nature trail car park at Coille na Glas-leitire
•PUBLIC TOILETS•	Beinn Eighe Visitor Centre, 1½ miles (2.4km) south and at Kinlochewe

Walk 45 Directions

Beinn Eighe is Britain's oldest National Nature Reserve (1951) and the Mountain Trail is possibly Scotland's toughest nature trail. The route is well waymarked. From the end of the car park, turn left to pass under the road; immediately turn left again, following a sign for the Mountain Trail. The path goes under birches, with a stream on its right, then under pines. It then climbs slightly more steeply, across slabs of reddish sandstone, to the marker cairn named '**Pines**'.

Scots pines once clothed all the valley sides of Wester Ross. The ones around Loch Maree were fed into the fires of an iron works directly opposite and the furnaces at Bonawe near Oban. More recently, ancient pines were felled to make ammunition boxes during World War Two. Genetic analysis has shown that the pines here are related to those of France and Spain, whereas those in the

Cairngorms and eastern Scotland spread after the ice age from northern Europe.

> ***WHERE TO EAT AND DRINK***   ⓘ
> The **Loch Maree Hotel** serves excellent meals in its lounge bar and restaurant, surrounded by stuffed fish in glass cases. There are also several cafés and a hotel at Kinlochewe.

The path climbs more steeply up rough stone steps to a footbridge, and then up more steps with the stream on its right. Looking at the rocks under the small waterfalls, you'll see that the bedrock has changed from rounded red sandstone to angular pale-grey quartzite. From the cairn called '**Geology**' you can see all three of the distinctive rocks of Wester Ross. Quartzite is underfoot and over-head. Across **Loch Maree**, the steep-sided stack of Slioch is Torridonian sandstone, standing on a base of greyish Lewisian gneiss. Slioch is a remnant of a thick layer of sandstone laid at a time when Scotland was under an ocean; the

Walk 45

gneiss surface now uncovered represents a landscape that first felt the air 500 million years ago.

The gneiss and sandstone date from long before multi-celled life on earth. The younger quartzite on top shows some of the oldest fossils and at the cairn called 'Trumpet Rock' you can see some of them. These are the trumpet-shaped entrances of worm-holes made when the rock was still sea-bottom sludge.

WHAT TO LOOK FOR ⓘ

From the top of the trail there's a chance of seeing a **golden eagle**. It may fly from one side of the sky to the other without flapping its wings at all, gaining height by soaring in thermals of rising air.

The cairn called '**305m**' indicates the 1,000ft mark. Above, you can see how the quartzite, originally laid in flat layers on a sea bed, now dips fairly steeply towards Loch Maree. The path passes along the base of a crag, then turns up left to a cairn called '**Heather**'. At the cairn called '**460m**' (about 1,500ft) you can see white marks the size of a thumb-print. These are the same worm-holes as at Trumpet Rock, but further in, away from the entrances. This 'pipe rock' layer is found all over Wester Ross.

The **Conservation Cairn** marks the high point of the path and has a fine view up to Beinn Eighe. The rotten quartzite pinnacles, called the Black Carls, are seen more clearly from Kinlochewe. Their serrated outline gives the mountain its name, the Hill of the File.

Here the path turns right into a hummocky landscape of rocks and gravel that's still very much as the glaciers left it. You go down steps to

pass a lochan, then reach another called **Lunar Loch**. The path now heads downhill – the descent is not quite so steep as the climb.

Below the **305m cairn** you cross a dry stream bed to a knoll with a fine view along Loch Maree. The heather here is suddenly deeper, representing a narrow belt of mineral-rich bedrock, and just below you can see the rock itself at the **Fossil Cairn**. The fossils are in fact another sort of worm-hole.

The way descends to the left of the deep ravine of the **Allt na h-Airighe**. At the cairn called '**Ice Age**', quartzite slabs show the scratches of the glacier that moved down the valley towards the left. The marks show most clearly on the fresh surface exposed by recent feet.

Back in the forest, turn left at a path junction where the Woodland Trail rejoins. Shortly turn left. The short side-path ahead leads to a view-point cairn built in layers of quartzite, sandstone and gneiss. The path drops through the sheltering trees to reach and cross the **A832**, a fairly fast stretch of the road with poor visibility, so take care. The way continues along lakeside shingle on the right, to a footbridge leading back to the car park.

WHILE YOU'RE THERE ⓘ

Queen Victoria stayed at the Loch Maree Hotel, where a small **waterfall** was named after her. A path leads up to it from a car park on the lochside road, or a slightly longer forest walk from Slatterdale. Far above, the river divides into two branches, half of it heading west for Gairloch. Locals suspect this unusual formation (grid ref 884676) is not natural, but a means of improving the waterfall ready for the queen's visit.

Into Scotland's Great Wilderness

A pleasant walk around Loch Kernsary and down the Ewe – the country's shortest river.

•DISTANCE•	6½ miles (10.4km)
•MINIMUM TIME•	2hrs 45min
•ASCENT / GRADIENT•	250ft (76m)
•LEVEL OF DIFFICULTY•	
•PATHS•	Mostly good, but one short rough, wet section, 3 stiles
•LANDSCAPE•	Moorland and loch side
•SUGGESTED MAP•	aqua3 OS Explorer 434 Gairloch & Loch Ewe
•START / FINISH•	Grid reference: NG 857808
•DOG FRIENDLINESS•	Close control on moorland and tracks carrying estate traffic
•PARKING•	In Poolewe, just up B8057 side street
•PUBLIC TOILETS•	At start

BACKGROUND TO THE WALK

As you walk inland from Poolewe, you're entering one of the largest empty areas in the United Kingdom. Turn left instead of right at Kernsary Farm, and you can walk for two full days before you reach any road.

Great Wilderness

On the slight rise before Loch Kernsary, you get a surprise view right into the heart of this mountain wonderland. At the back of the view is A'Mhaighdean, the Maiden, Scotland's most remote mountain. It takes half a day's walk to get to this hill from anywhere. That walk will be along the edges of long dark lochs and under some very large crags. Beinn Lair has a quartzite cliff with an evil north-face gleam that's 3 miles (4.8km) wide, as big as the north face of Ben Nevis, but a whole lot less visited.

Behind A'Mhaighdean is An Teallach, called the Forge because of the cloudy vapours that stream across its semicircular ridge – imagine plunging a red hot sword into a water bucket. That ridge has great lumpy towers to scramble round, 3ft-wide (1m) ridges to walk along and an edge that if you fall off it will take about four seconds before you land on anything at all.

The Letterewe Accord

All this belongs to a gentleman from Holland called Paul van Vlissingen. In 1993 he signed an agreement with the Mountaineering Council of Scotland that first set out the principle of responsible access for all. Deer stalking restrictions would be only on days when deer stalking was actually taking place – a step forward when walkers were sometimes threatened with high-velocity rifle fire from August to February. The estate also undertook not to build any new landrover tracks. As a result, business here is carried out on foot, by boat and by pony. This Letterewe Accord has become the foundation of the new century's access legislation.

Rights of Way

The paths used on this walk are, as it happens, established rights of way. Even so, you'll notice a sudden change about halfway along the side of Loch Kernsary. The first part of the path has been rebuilt by the National Trust for Scotland, using their members' annual subscriptions. One new member pays for about 2ft (60cm) of path. At the edge of their land the repairs stop, mid-bog.

In Scotland, no one is obliged to build or maintain footpaths. The surprising thing, if you walk all 50 of these walks, is how many people are doing it anyway. Paths in this book are looked after by charities such as the John Muir Trust, by Scottish Natural Heritage and Forest Enterprise, by private landowners in Argyll and Atholl, by regional and community councils and groups of ordinary walkers.

Walk 46 Directions

① A kissing gate beside the public toilets leads to a path that crosses the **Marie Curie Field of Hope** to the main road. Turn left to cross the bridge over the **River Ewe** and then head all the way through the village. At the 40mph derestriction sign, there's a white cottage on the right. Beside it, a tarred trackway has a Scottish Rights of Way Society signpost for Kernsary.

② Follow the track over a cattle grid to a new track that forks off to the left. After 50yds (46m), keep ahead on a path with a wall on its left. It passes through a kissing gate into **Cnoc na Lise**, the Garden Hill. This has been replanted as a community wood with oak and birch trees. Another kissing gate leads out of the young wood. The good, reconstructed path runs over some bare sandstone slabs and under a low-voltage power line. It crosses a low spur to a fine view of Loch Kernsary and the remote, steep-sided hills of the Great Wilderness, then goes over a stream to the loch side.

WHAT TO LOOK FOR ℹ️

The River Ewe may be short, but it's very full of **salmon**. As well as stony piers for anglers, you'll see artificial rapids where partial dams force the water into a central channel. Salmon will lie up in the pools below, waiting for rain to fill up the river, instead of proceeding immediately into Loch Maree.

---

③ The path follows the left-hand shore of the loch, passing through patches of birch scrub. About half-way along the loch, it suddenly deteriorates, becoming a braided trod of boulder and bog. From a stile at the loch head, slant to the left down a meadow to find a footbridge under an oak tree. Head up, with a fence on your right, to join a track beside **Kernsary farm**.

WHERE TO EAT AND DRINK ℹ️

The **Poolewe Hotel** was the original village inn. It has a restaurant, with fine sunset views, and offers bar meals in the lounge bar (children are welcome, but not dogs). Opposite the car park is the **Bridge House Coffee Shop and Gallery**. The **Pool House Hotel** has an upmarket restaurant called North by Northwest.

---

④ Turn right, through a gate. Follow the track past the farm, to a culvert crossing of the **Kernsary River**. This becomes a ford only after heavy rain. If needed, you will find a footbridge 70yds (64m) upstream. After crossing, turn right on a smooth track. The new track bears left, away from Loch Kernsary towards the hollow containing Loch Maree. After the bridge over the **Inveran River** is a gate with a ladder stile. Signs welcoming responsible walkers (and even cyclists) reflect the principles of the Letterewe Accord. Soon come the first views of Loch Maree. The driveway of **Inveran house** joins from the left and the track starts being tarred.

⑤ At a sign, 'Blind Corners', a green track on the left leads down to the point where the narrow loch imperceptibly becomes a wide river. Return to the main track and follow it above and then beside the **River Ewe**. It reaches **Poolewe** just beside the bridge.

WHILE YOU'RE THERE ℹ️

One of Scotland's greatest gardens lies beside the Great Wilderness. In 1862, the Gairloch Mackenzies found themselves free of feuding Macleods and MacDonalds and turned their attention to gardening. Osgood Mackenzie planted trees to create shelter belts against the salt winds, improved (or rather, created) the soil using vast quantities of seaweed hauled up from the beach by basket, and found that the mild western climate would grow exotic plants from Chile and South Africa. Now managed by the National Trust for Scotland, **Inverewe Garden** is one of Ross-shire's most surprising and popular attractions.

Walk 47

Farigaig Forest and Loch Ness

Overlooking Loch Ness and past the home of a different monster, the Beast of Boleskine.

•DISTANCE•	4¼ miles (6.8km)
•MINIMUM TIME•	2hrs 15min
•ASCENT / GRADIENT•	700ft (213m) ▲▲▲
•LEVEL OF DIFFICULTY•	🚶🚶 🚶🚶 🚶
•PATHS•	Waymarked paths and tracks, no stiles
•LANDSCAPE•	Hillside of mixed woodland
•SUGGESTED MAP•	aqua3 OS Explorer 416 Inverness, Loch Ness & Culloden
•START / FINISH•	Grid reference: NH 522237
•DOG FRIENDLINESS•	On leads for short stretch past Easter Boleskine
•PARKING•	Forest Enterprise car park
•PUBLIC TOILETS•	At start

BACKGROUND TO THE WALK

With so many fine sights in Scotland, it's a shame that such large numbers of people take the trouble to see one that doesn't actually exist. The first encounter with the Loch Ness monster was back to the 6th century AD, when St Columba was crossing the River Ness. One of his companions was attacked by a water beast. When the saint ordered it to go away, it did. The onlookers, pagan barbarians whose friend had already been eaten, promptly converted to Christianity. The account was set down 100 years later by Adomnan, an abbot of Iona. It sounds suspiciously like an earlier incident from the life of a different holy man, St Martin of Tours, and also like a story about how Christianity took over a site where human sacrifice had been offered to a river god.

Later confirmation came during the Lisbon earthquake of 1755. A shock wave, freakishly magnified along Loch Ness, sent breakers crashing against the shore at Fort Augustus – clearly Columba's monster was still down there disturbing the water.

The Beast of Boleskine

Authentic sightings of a rather different monster did, however, taken place along this walk in the early 1900s. Finding it fashionable to be Scottish, Alexander Crowley changed his name to Alesteir and bought the nearby hall to become the Laird of Boleskine. In his time, Crowley was known as 'The Beast of Boleskine', the 'wickedest man alive'. He identified himself with the Great Beast described in the final book of the Bible, the seven-headed monster that was to battle with the angels at the end of time. In pursuit of his precept 'do what thou wilt shall be the whole of the law', he debauched minor film stars, betrayed his friends and became an alcoholic and heroin addict. At Boleskine, as he studied his magical grimoires, the sky darkened at midday so that candles had to be lit, and the lodge keeper went mad. We might take the darkening of the sky as a normal Scottish summer raincloud, but we can still see the rowan trees that his neighbours planted to protect themselves from his magical influence.

Apart from seducing his neighbours and brightening the Inverness-shire scene with various exotic mistresses, Crowley contributed to local life by prankishly reporting to the Society for the Suppression of Vice the prevalence of prostitution in Foyers (where there wasn't any). He also made an impassioned plea against the plan to enclose the Falls of Foyers in hydro-electric water pipes.

Walk 47 Directions

① From the car park follow yellow waymarkers uphill near a stream. After 100yds (91m), a path on the right is signed 'Loch View'. After a bench, the path contours briefly then turns up left, to a higher viewpoint. It then turns back sharply right and descends on earth steps through a little crag to a forest road. Turn right for 200yds (183m).

② Turn up left on a footpath with more yellow waymarkers. The path has a low, heavily mossed wall alongside as it bends up to a higher forest road. Turn right and walk for about 150yds (137m) until you reach a sharp left-hand bend. Keep ahead here, on a small footpath through an area of cleared forestry, then go steeply up to the left under trees. At the top, bear left along a little ridge, dropping gently downhill to a viewpoint.

WHAT TO LOOK FOR ⓘ

The only half-convincing photo of the **monster** shows it with a long neck, small head and a single hump. (It may be a telephoto shot of a swimming grass snake.) But if you do believe in monsters, keep your camera out of its case and make sure it's one with real film – a digital image isn't going to convince anybody.

③ Return for 100yds (91m) and bear left down the other side of the ridge. The path descends steeply to a forest road. A sign indicates **Lochan Torr an Tuill**, near by on the right, with a picnic table.

④ Return down the forest road, past where you joined it. It climbs gently, then descends to the sharp right bend where you turned off earlier – the waymarker says 'to Car Park' on the side now facing you. After 150yds (137m), at another 'to Car Park' waymarker, turn left down the path with the low mossed wall to the forest road below (Point ②). Turn left, past a red/green waymarker. The track kinks left past a quarry.

WHERE TO EAT AND DRINK ⓘ

Craigdarroch House Hotel at Lower Foyers is an upmarket country house, but it offers very good bar meals at normal bar prices. Its restaurant is a pleasingly leaky conservatory with views of Loch Ness. The **Falls of Foyers Tea and Coffee Shop** is in Upper Foyers, at the top of the path to the waterfall.

⑤ Where the main track bends right, downhill, keep ahead on a green track with a red/green waymarker. It emerges from the trees at a signpost. Follow this down to the right towards **Easter Boleskine house**. Green waymarkers indicate a diversion to the left of the house, to join its driveway track below. Follow this down to the **B852**.

⑥ Turn right for 50yds (46m). Below the left edge of the road is a tarred track. Turn down past a blue/green waymarker to cross this track, with two blue waymarkers leading into a path beyond. This passes down to the right of electricity transformers. At the foot of the slope, the main path bears right with a blue waymarker. It runs above the loch shore and joins a gravel track just below **Lower Birchwood House**. At a tarmac turning circle, an overgrown jetty on the left is great for monster-watchers. The tarred lane ahead leads up to the **B852**, with the car park just above on the right.

WHILE YOU'RE THERE ⓘ

The **Falls of Foyers** are reached by a short but quite exciting walk from Upper Foyers. In September 1803, the poet Samuel Taylor Coleridge wrote about them – 'The plumage of the fall, the puffs of smoke in every direction from the bed of plumy foam at the bottom, the restless network of waves on its pool.' Although the stream above has now been dammed for the Foyers Power Station, a reasonable spell of wet weather leaves plenty of water for the fall. Otherwise you can see it in an old print in the bar of the Craigdarroch House Hotel.

The Falls of Rogie

From a Victorian spa to a salmon-leaping waterfall.

•DISTANCE•	10 miles (16.1km)
•MINIMUM TIME•	5hrs
•ASCENT / GRADIENT•	1,200ft (365m) ▲▲▲
•LEVEL OF DIFFICULTY•	🚶 🚶 🚶
•PATHS•	Waymarked paths and track, no stiles
•LANDSCAPE•	Plantation, wild forest and riverside
•SUGGESTED MAP•	aqua3 OS Explorer 437 Ben Wyvis & Strathpeffer
•START / FINISH•	Grid reference: NH 483582
•DOG FRIENDLINESS•	On lead for section past Loch Kinellan
•PARKING•	Main square, Strathpeffer
•PUBLIC TOILETS•	At start, Contin (Point ④) and Falls of Rogie car parks

BACKGROUND TO THE WALK

Stand on the suspension bridge at Falls of Rogie between July and September, at a time when the river's fairly full, and you might catch a glimpse of the silver flash of a leaping salmon. It's a thrilling sight to see a 3ft (1m) long fish attempting to swim up against the force of the water. Eventually it'll make it, or else discover the easy way round – the fish ladder carved out of the rock on the right-hand side. But if you'd been here 200 years ago, that single salmon would have been a dozen or even a hundred. During the autumn run, the falls must have appeared almost to flow in reverse, an upstream current of flashing fish.

The Rise and Fall of the Salmon

Salmon was once food for the taking, like blackberries today. You went down to the river and took as many as you thought you could eat. Smoked above the peat fire of the black houses, it was a staple food through the winter. Farm workers even used their industrial muscle to demand that they shouldn't be obliged to eat salmon more than three times a week.

Today, however, this majestic fish is steadily heading towards extinction. In the last ten years, the catch in Scotland's rivers has shrunk from 1,200 tons to 200. The main reason has been netting in the estuaries, and in their feeding grounds around the Arctic pack ice. Angling clubs have bought up and discontinued estuary netting rights. The international community still squabbles on about the Arctic drift nets, and now a new danger to wild fish is posed by parasites and disease leaking out of the sea cages of Scotland's 340 fish farms.

Egg, fry, alevin, parr, smolt, salmon, kelt – these are the seven ages of the salmon's extraordinary life. For one or two years it behaves like a trout, hanging in the still water behind a boulder and waiting for food to float by. But then in one of nature's changes, as striking in its way as a caterpillar becoming a butterfly or a tadpole becoming a frog, its scales become silver and it turns downstream, totally altering its body chemistry for life in the salt water. Its new name of 'smolt' is probably a reference to silver poured from the furnace. Four or five years later, now called a salmon, it returns. We don't know how it navigates from Greenland back to the Cromarty Firth. Once back in Scotland, it identifies the outflow of the Conon by the taste of the water and works its way upstream, taking all the correct turnings to the patch of gravel where it was once an egg and an alevin.

Walk

48

Walk 48 **Directions**

① Head along the main road towards **Contin**. When you reach the edge of the town, turn right at a signpost for Garve then, at a bend in the lane, turn left, following another signpost.

② Pass round to the left of **Loch Kinellan**, then keep ahead up a faint path through gorse to the corner of a plantation. Here you join a larger track leading into the forest. After another ¼ mile (400m) it reaches a signpost.

③ Turn left for **View Rock** on a good path with green waymarkers. At View Rock, a side-path diverts to the right for the viewpoint. After a steep descent, ignore a green path turning off to the left and follow green waymarkers downhill. At a forest road turn left, then back right for 60yds (55m) to a path on the left. It crosses another forest road to a car park.

④ At the end of the car park you'll pick up a wide path signed 'River Walk'. After a stream culvert, the main path bends up to the right, past a waymark with a roe deer head to a forest road. Turn left, signposted 'Garve', and in another 80yds (73m) bear left, heading slightly downhill.

⑤ Go on for 600yds (549m), when a small track on the left is signed 'Falls of Rogie'. At its foot, cross a spectacular footbridge below the falls and turn right, upstream. The path has green waymarkers and after ¼ mile (400m) bends left away from the river. It crosses rocky ground to a junction. Turn up right, to a car park.

⑥ Leave the car park through a wooden arch and follow green waymarkers back to the bridge. Retrace the outward route to Point ⑤ and turn sharp left up another forest road. It leads uphill to a four-way junction.

> **WHILE YOU'RE THERE** ⓘ
> The **Highland Museum of Childhood** at Strathpeffer is in the Victorian station building. Its displays on the life of children include serious social history, but also some delightful photographs. There is a toy collection, with fine wax dolls, and hands-on toys for younger visitors.

⑦ Turn right on a smaller track to pass between obstructing boulders, then left on a rutted path to rejoin the same track higher up. After 600yds (549m) it reaches the signpost at Point ③. Keep ahead and retrace the outward route to Point ②. Turn left on the tarred lane, which becomes a track. Keep ahead towards a house, but before it, turn left through a kissing gate, with a second one beyond leading into a plantation with a signpost for Strathpeffer.

⑧ Follow the main track ahead until you see **Strathpeffer** down on the right. At the next junction bear right down the wood edge and turn right into the town. The street on the left leads past a church with a square steeple, where you turn down right to the main square.

> **WHERE TO EAT AND DRINK** ⓘ
> **Bluebells Tearoom** at Strathpeffer is in the old spa buildings opposite the Pavilion, a few steps from the end of the walk. The **Highland Museum of Childhood** has a station-platform café with home-baked scones. Another such **café**, at Dingwall, is open year-round and welcomes dogs on the platform.

Cnoc Mor and Knock Farril

A grassy ridge walk above Strathpeffer to a vitrified fort.
See map and information panel for Walk 48

•DISTANCE•	6 miles (9.7km)
•MINIMUM TIME•	2hrs 45min
•ASCENT / GRADIENT•	1,066ft (325m) ▲▲▲
•LEVEL OF DIFFICULTY•	🚶🚶 🚶

Walk 49 Directions (Walk 48 option)

From the car park, turn left down the main street towards the **Ben Wyvis Hotel**. Pass the hotel grounds and turn right, up a steep lane. Bear right, continuing up the hill, now on a grassy path towards the edge of the woods. Cross a stile to the maze, Point Ⓐ.

The maze shows the rocks of Scotland. If you've done Walks 41 to 46 in Wester Ross, you will find some more Torridonian sandstone here; the Skye gabbro is missing, however. From the top of the maze, an avenue of stones leads up and to the left. Ignore a path forking up to the right, and keep ahead to join a track at a waymarker. This runs to the left, keeping the same level through a gate with a stile where it leaves the woods. It then rises gently to a four-way signpost in a col. Turn left up a slope dotted with conglomerate rocks to the hill fort of Knock Farril, Point Ⓑ. The first knob of ruined stonework on the left shows the vitrified rocks, thought to be caused by a fire that destroyed the fort's wooden palisade. Return to the four-way sign and keep ahead for **Cnoc Mor**.

The path passes a bench and follows the ridge-line above. A sculpture with three faces was a gift from Armenia to local schoolchildren who raised money after the earthquake there in December 1988. At the next col keep ahead through a kissing gate and over a stile, signed for Cnoc Mor. A path, with a fence on its right, leads over a preliminary knoll and up to the **trig point** (Point Ⓒ).

Go down alongside the fence for another few steps, then turn left in an overgrown track. This spirals round the hill to a signpost pointing towards you. Here a path on the right contours round the hill to another signpost. Keep ahead for **Jamestown**. At the forest edge, turn down left and follow a fence through a tree strip before crossing a stile on the right (Point Ⓓ).

Continue downhill just inside the wood to pass houses at the edge of Jamestown. At a waymarker the path bends right to follow the wood's foot. After ½ mile (800m) the path forks, with the right-hand branch running under pines to a car park (Point Ⓔ). Walk through here to the access road and follow this out to the main road. Turn right and walk down the hill on the pavement into **Strathpeffer**.

Walk 50

River Islands of Inverness

An Inverness town walk of riverside, seaside and canalside.

•DISTANCE•	7 miles (11.3km)
•MINIMUM TIME•	3hrs
•ASCENT / GRADIENT•	197ft (60m) ▲ ▲ ▲
•LEVEL OF DIFFICULTY•	🚶 🚶 🚶
•PATHS•	Smooth and wide, no stiles
•LANDSCAPE•	City and foreshore
•SUGGESTED MAP•	aqua3 OS Explorer 416 Inverness, Loch Ness & Culloden
•START / FINISH•	Grid reference: NH 664447
•DOG FRIENDLINESS•	Forbidden on Tomnahuirich and Whin Island – see alternative routes
•PARKING•	Pay-and-display in Bishop Street, south of cathedral
•PUBLIC TOILETS•	Whin Park and beside Inverness Castle

Walk 50 Directions

Head up **Ness Walk**, with the river on your right, passing opposite the castle. Stay on the left-hand bank past a road bridge (it leads to the tourist information centre). Pass the **Glenalbyn Bar** into **Huntley Street** to a suspension footbridge.

Cross this, to the foot of **Church Lane**. At the other end of this short street is **Dunbar's Hospital**, a handsome building from 1688. Return to the river and continue downstream, with the water on your left. A cycleway leads under the ugly concrete bridge of the A82.

WHERE TO EAT AND DRINK ℹ️
Near the start of the walk, the **Glenalbyn Bar** is a former 1700s coaching inn, refurbished in traditional Scottish 1950s style. It serves snacks, but does not welcome dogs. Just after joining the canal, you pass **Canal Kebabs** (which also serves fish suppers) and the **Caley Inn**. This bar, which offers snacks, is two tiny upstairs rooms of a cottage.

Turn left across the **Waterloo Bridge**, built in 1896, then right on **Anderson Street** and continue alongside the river, passing under a railway bridge.

Continue along the streets nearest the river, passing two branches of the **Gael Force Superstore**. Beyond it you regain the river as it opens into the **Beauly Firth**. Behind a pumping station, a short track leads to a beacon. This has a fine view of the estuary and Kessock Bridge.

Continue along the shore to the old ferry slipway – you'll notice the corresponding slipway on the opposite shore. A sea wall path ahead runs above a seaweed expanse, where at low tide you will see curlews and sandpipers. After a level crossing, the path passes between salt pools to the **Caledonian Canal**.

On the right, lock keepers' cottages and a lighthouse mark the canal's entry into the salt water. Your route turns left, past the wide **Muirtown**

Basin (which should be on your right). You pass a swing bridge, with **Canal Kebabs** on the left and then the **Caley Inn**. The canal now rises through a set of locks. Follow it for another ¾ mile (1.2km) to a gate, with a swing bridge visible ahead.

Those with dogs must continue along the tow path to this swing bridge, those without can turn off left just before the gate, on a tarred path. The street ahead runs to the left of the wooded hill which is the **Tomnahuirich Cemetery**. A gate between white pillars lets you in. The cemetery is closed at night and dogs are forbidden.

For the most atmospheric path up, bear right inside the gates, then left on to a path under a lime tree. This joins a track at its hairpin bend. Go round left to rediscover the path at a tall birch. After 50yds (46m), turn left up a rhododendron tunnel. The path winds up the steep end of the hill, with several flights of steps. Across the top of the hill runs a gravestone avenue, dipping into an amphitheatre and ending at a war memorial with a fine view.

Return to the amphitheatre and turn right, on to a track that bends back around the hill. At the prow of the hill, turn left down steep steps to exit from the cemetery close to the swing bridge of the **Caledonian Canal** mentioned earlier.

WHILE YOU'RE THERE ℹ️

Inverness Museum and Art Gallery is just up from the information centre close to the start of the walk. Next door is the castle. If you didn't see the dolphins on your walk, cross Kessock Bridge to the North Kessock Seal and Dolphin Centre where you're guaranteed a sighting, and you can hear them via hydrophones.

Turn right to the swing bridge, but don't cross it; turn left along the nearside tow path. (Those with dogs must turn more sharply left here to follow the waymarkers of the Great Glen Way.) After ½ mile (800m), the **River Ness** appears below. Turn left on a path that runs past a rugby pitch to a footbridge to **Whin Island**. Again, dogs aren't allowed in this park.

WHAT TO LOOK FOR ℹ️

The 130 **bottlenose dolphins** in the Moray Firth are the world's most northerly population. The narrows under Kessock Bridge are a common dolphin-spotting location. Because it's so cold, Moray dolphins are bigger and fatter than elsewhere in the world. The population is about half the size necessary for long-term viability and is declining each year. Those with binoculars might also spot seals, porpoises or whales.

Turn left on any path along the island, passing to the right of the ornamental pool to a path with the main river close by on the right. At the park's end is a footbridge which leads back to the left-hand bank of the river.

Turn right, downstream. This is again the **Great Glen Way**, where dogs and their owners rejoin the route. A tarred riverside path leads to a white suspension bridge. Cross to the first of the **Ness Islands** and turn left. At its end, another footbridge leads to a second island, and at the end of that, a further footbridge leads to the other bank of the river.

Turn left to continue downstream for another 650yds (594m). A final footbridge leads back across the river, with the cathedral ¼ mile (400m) downstream.

Walking in Safety

All these walks are suitable for any reasonably fit person, but less experienced walkers should try the easier walks first. Route finding is usually straightforward, but you will find that an Ordnance Survey map is a useful addition to the route maps and descriptions.

Risks

Although each walk here has been researched with a view to minimising the risks to the walkers who follow its route, no walk in the countryside can be considered to be completely free from risk. Walking in the outdoors will always require a degree of common sense and judgement to ensure that it is as safe as possible.

- Be particularly careful on cliff paths and in upland terrain, where the consequences of a slip can be very serious.

- Remember to check tidal conditions before walking on the seashore.

- Some sections of route are by, or cross, busy roads. Take care and remember traffic is a danger even on minor country lanes.

- Be careful around farmyard machinery and livestock, especially if you have children with you.

- Be aware of the consequences of changes in the weather and check the forecast before you set out. Carry spare clothing and a torch if you are walking in the winter months. Remember the weather can change very quickly at any time of the year, and in moorland and heathland areas, mist and fog can make route finding much harder. Don't set out in these conditions unless you are confident of your navigation skills in poor visibility. In summer remember to take account of the heat and sun; wear a hat and carry spare water.

- On walks away from centres of population you should carry a whistle and survival bag. If you do have an accident requiring the emergency services, make a note of your position as accurately as possible and dial 999.

Acknowledgements

Ronald Turnbull thanks the following for their help and advice: John Ireland, Forestry Commission; Peter Duncan, SNH Craig Meagaidh; Ordnance Survey Press Office; Charlie and Priscilla Rose, Alligin; Margaret at Grantown Museum and many others who answered emails or were patient on the phone. The paths in this book are provided and maintained by many organisations, including Atholl Estates, Crown Estates at Glenlivet, Flowerdale Estate, The Footpath Trust (Dingwall), Forest Enterprise, Highland Council, Inveraray Estate, John Muir Trust*, Kinlochleven Land Development Trust, The National Trust for Scotland*, Perth & Kinross Council, Raasay Social Services, Rothiemurchus Estate, Scottish Natural Heritage, The Scottish Rights of Way and Access Society*, Upper Deeside Access Trust. Join one of the organisations marked with an asterisk to help fund their future work.

AQUA3 AA Publishing and Outcrop Publishing Services would like to thank Chartech for supplying aqua3 maps for this book.
For more information visit their website: www.aqua3.com

Series management: Outcrop Publishing Services Limited, Cumbria
Series editor: Chris Bagshaw
Front cover: AA Photo Library/S Day **Back cover:** AA Photo Library/J Martin